WHEN MEN HOLD POWER THEY ABUSE IT

THERE'S A CONTINUOUS ROUND OF REVELATIONS ABOUT SEXUAL ABUSE FROM MEN, WHETHER IT'S IN HOLLYWOOD, BIG BUSINESS OR CHARITIES AND EVERYONE SAYS, 'THIS IS OUTRAGEOUS.' BUT I'M THINKING, 'HOW LONG WILL IT BE BEFORE WE GET THE MESSAGE THAT WHEN MEN HOLD POWER THEY ABUSE IT?'

First published in 2019 by Martin Firrell Company Ltd.
10 Queen Street Place, London EC4R 1AG, United Kingdom.

ISBN 978-1-912622-13-9

Devised and edited by Martin Firrell.

© Copyright Martin Firrell Company 2019.

All rights reserved. No part of this publication may be reproduced, stored in or introduced into a retrieval system, or transmitted, in any form, or by any means (electronic, mechanical, photocopying, recording or otherwise) without the prior written consent of the publisher.

This book is sold subject to the condition that it shall not, by way of trade or otherwise, be lent, re-sold, hired out, or otherwise circulated without the publisher's prior consent in any form of binding or cover other than that in which it is published and without a similar condition including this condition being imposed on the subsequent purchaser.

Text is set in Baskerville, 11pt on 17pt.

Baskerville is a serif typeface designed in 1754 by John Baskerville (1706-1775) in Birmingham, England. Compared to earlier typeface designs, Baskerville increased the contrast between thick and thin strokes. Serifs were made sharper and more tapered, and the axis of rounded letters was placed in a more vertical position. The curved strokes were made more circular in shape, and the characters became more regular.

Baskerville is categorised as a transitional typeface between classical typefaces and high contrast modern faces. Of his own typeface, John Baskerville wrote, 'Having been an early admirer of the beauty of letters, I became insensibly desirous of contributing to the perfection of them. I formed to myself ideas of greater accuracy than had yet appeared, and had endeavoured to produce a set of types according to what I conceived to be their true proportion.'

ANNIE RICKARD

Annie Rickard is the former Global President of media company Posterscope Worldwide and a member of the Steering Committee and Executive Committee of the Women's Equality Party (WEP).

She began her career in out of home advertising media (OOH) more than 30 years ago at British Posters. The company was originally formed by two large advertising agencies, J. Walter Thomson (JWT) and Collet, Dickinson, Pearce (CDP), to market their poster holdings jointly.

She went on to co-found Harrison, Salinson and Company, one of the first specialist media agencies to plan and buy short term poster campaigns tailored to the needs of individual advertisers.

In 1982, Annie Rickard rebranded Harrison Salinson as Posterscope UK. She grew the company into a global network of over 1,000 people in 57 offices around the world. She served in the roles of global CEO, and Global President of Posterscope Worldwide from 2001 to 2018.

Out of home is one of the few traditional media channels to have benefitted from the digital revolution. More than half the poster sites in developed markets are now digital. Posterscope was at the centre of this modernisation, redefining the poster medium through its investment in data, technology and people.

Annie Rickard succeeded in a sector that was, for most of her career, dominated by men. She was one of the chief architects of the out of home media revolution.

TRANSCRIPT

Annie Rickard, founder and former Global President Posterscope Worldwide, in conversation with public artist Martin Firrell, 23 April 2018.

— Martin Firrell: **When did you have your first inkling that there were power imbalances related to being a woman or a man?**

— **Annie Rickard:** I went to work for an organisation called British Posters. It was the sales and marketing arm for eight different media owners. The board of the company was entirely male and my first experience of the abuse of power was there. It was very noticeable in the way they interacted with women. My boss was a woman. She'd taken over from a man and she was doing the same job he did but without the same status. She was allowed into the boardroom to talk about the sales figures then she'd have to leave the meeting and they would invite her for drinks afterwards. Her predecessor, who in my opinion was less bright, less able and less capable, was part of that board simply because he was a man. So that was my first real experience of inequality.

— **And what was your woman boss like to you?**

— She was really, really supportive. She was a very independent woman who never married and seemed very much in control of her life and her relationships with men. She was very, very supportive of me and we're still close to this day. I don't know if she would call herself a feminist but I'm now hearing her question the basis on which men held so much power for so long. These days, she mentors lots of young women. She might not have thought of herself as a feminist but I think she is.

— **That observation that men held so much power: what were the characteristics of that power-holding at the time?**

— First of all I could see it in relation to my boss. She was not considered their equal. The board behaved very badly towards the rest of us. When you were invited to socialise with them they made you feel very uncomfortable. They were not afraid to use their status to make a pass at you physically, or lunge at you in a taxi, or stick their hands on your breasts. It was quite blatant and quite shocking. They just saw that as a right of theirs. They didn't express any interest in you as an individual. They didn't talk about your career or what you'd done for the business. They were just having their fun.

— **They were playing with their power and you.**

— Yes. I can remember my boss came to see me and she said, 'The board would like you to join them for drinks. I'm going as well.' And I said, 'No, thank you.' And she was surprised because it was meant to be an honour. I said, 'I don't want to. I don't want to socialise with those men. I'm not interested.' It didn't even cross my mind that it might be something you should do to help your career.

— **Where were you born?**

— I was born in north London, in Neasden. I spent a year in Dublin at about the age of 20 but apart from that I've always worked in London. I went to school in Harrow which is where I returned to live. My dad came over from Ireland and worked as a plasterer and then a foreman and then set up his own building business. There was a sense of improving oneself and that's quite possibly what drove me to work hard at school. I enjoyed history and English literature and so on. I enjoyed learning. For me there was an element of 'cracking on with it'. I was the eldest daughter of five children, and in that situation there's an expectation that you're going to be a 'good girl', work hard, help the family.

— **What was your mother like as a role model?**

— She was of her time so she never really worked once she had children. I remember having my first child, Thomas, when I was 37. It seemed inconceivable to go back to work, go back to presenting to people and being professional when I was the mother of this little thing. Those two worlds just seemed so far apart. I remember my mum saying to me, 'At this stage, and for the next year, it's really just about getting him fed and changed - so you should go back. Financial independence is really important and it's something I never had. If you don't like it you can always stop and no harm will have been done.' I thought this was very wise advice considering she'd had no personal experience of that kind of situation.

— Were you ambitious? Did you have dreams of being very successful?

— I certainly didn't want to live in the same way my parents did: living in a house, in a row of houses, having children and just sort of carrying on. I wanted to be different. That was part of my motivation for working hard at school. I wanted to find a different way or to find a way out. It's easy sometimes to attribute things retrospectively but I think I did want to be different. I wanted to live a different sort of life.

— What was your first job?

— I signed on to be a trainee underwriter at an insurance company. They were very excited about having me and they were fast-tracking me, and it was a very good salary. I left after the third week. I remember going to see the boss and saying, 'Look, I'm really sorry, but I've made a terrible mistake.' He said, 'How do you know? You've only been here five minutes. I've been here thirty years.' So I escaped! I ended up working in the PR department of a company called Goya. It felt quite glamorous to be in the world of PR but in reality a lot of what I did was sending out standard letters to customers who were unhappy with the product. I did get to know a little bit about marketing and advertising, though, and I thought that was very, very interesting. When I left Goya, I took a temporary job in an advertising agency called Collett, Dickinson, Pearce (CDP). At the time, it was the hottest agency in London. There was a man running the media department called Mike Yershon and he was changing everything about media. He said, 'Look, I don't know what I'm going to do. I'm going to do something in the world of posters and I want you to do it with me, so just stay on and we'll do something.' He ended up starting a new business in posters, or 'out of home' as we now call it, with another agency and although I was only in a supporting role, I was exposed to the creation of a new business. I was surrounded by these very energetic pioneers who were changing the rules. Even when it came to the posters themselves, CDP were creating the kinds of ads that nobody had ever seen before. They created 'Wolf in Sheep's Clothing' for Fiat and famous work for Parker Pens and Pretty Polly and Heineken, all those still iconic posters. I remember saying, 'But does any of this really work?' And somebody took me round the entire agency to show me the different departments and what they did, explaining why they felt it did work and all the different steps in the process. Looking back, it was incredibly generous of them because they could have just dismissed my question. I was lucky to stumble into one of the best agencies in London with a very enlightened leader in the media department. Up until then, media departments had been pretty much in the basement and all the emphasis was on creative teams and account men. This was the beginning of the emergence of media as important in its own right. Strategic thinking in media was being valued for the first time. I left the agency to take on more of an executive role with a poster company. CDP completely understood my reasons for leaving. They said, 'Go! Sometimes you have to leave somewhere to get promoted, to learn, and then maybe one day you'll come back.' They understood that I needed to be seen as a junior executive somewhere new. CDP doesn't exist anymore which is a shame.

—— **I'm interested in the link from CDP and then into media and to Posterscope. I haven't quite joined up all the steps.**

— From CDP I went into the sales and marketing organisation called British Posters. That was where eight media owners sold collectively through one organisation. Rather absurdly it was closed down by the monopolies commission. British Posters had been set up because the vast majority of clients who used posters were on them all the time. They were mostly alcohol and cigarette brands. That meant, if you were Fiat cars, you couldn't get onto the medium easily. It was dominated by advertisers who booked poster sites for twelve months of the year. That's where British Posters came in. They collated the unsold inventory and packaged it for clients like Fiat. When the company was closed down, my boss Judith and I felt that there was an opportunity to create a new kind of business that offered a bespoke service to advertisers. Computers had arrived in offices and that meant it would be possible to put together at short notice what we called 'short term advertising'. That would really open up the market and therefore it would also deliver growth, which it did. Posters accounted for about 3 or 4% of total advertising spend and nowadays it's 9 or 10%. Other companies followed us, setting up to offer short term advertising. Those companies that were set up to handle the long term displays had to change and become more like us. We were really disruptive.

— **Did you feel trepidation about risk?**

— No, because I was in my late 20s so I had absolutely nothing to lose. I loved the idea of setting up a business. There was myself and Judith and an older man. Judith and I got together with the idea of setting something up and then he had a similar idea. He knew Judith and contacted her. She said, 'Well, I'm already in talks with Annie, do you want to join us?' And that's what happened. Because he was older and richer, he ended up being the dominant shareholder. At that time we called it after him and Judith so it was called Harrison, Salinson and Company and I was the 'and Company'. Then when we sold it and they left, that's when I renamed it Posterscope. We had to work really, really, really hard for a long time. But it was very exciting. We went out and talked to people and asked for their business and created this company out of nothing.

— **How did it become your job to lead?**

— The company was about seven years old when it was sold. During that seven years, David would have seen himself as the boss rather than as an equal partner. But he was more involved with the financial side of the business and less with clients and the day-to-day operations. He saw himself as the figurehead and was a man of his time - status conscious and with firm opinions on everything.

— **Was that how your leadership emerged - because you were bringing in the business and you were operational?**

— Yes.

— **Did you look at yourself in the mirror one day and say, 'This is it. I'm going to step up and lead,' or did it just happen and suddenly you were leading?**

— I realised people wanted someone to make decisions and take that position of risk and occupy that position of authority.

— Were you aware of the responsibility and how did it sit with you?

— I remember thinking we should do Investors In People.[1] At the same time, I was apprehensive because it would put me in quite a vulnerable position. I would be getting a lot of feedback from people and, up until then, I'd been doing what I intuitively thought was right. It turned out to be a really important exercise because it gave me the confidence to go forward. Over those few years, I made the shift from being an owner, who knew what she was doing on a daily basis, to somebody who was letting go of the day-to-day operation and concentrating on leading the company and looking ahead. That was a real shift and I did feel hugely responsible for every single person. I felt very aware that all those people were depending on me.

— A lot of people talk about the difference between having a female or a male boss. But what about your experience of interacting with a board of men, the invitation to drinks etc, and then suddenly you are the board and you're interacting with men where you hold the power?

— I was just concentrating on doing the work. It was a while before I realised that there was one individual in particular (who I'd been supporting and promoting) who was not supporting me as much as I had thought. He had a sense of entitlement but that took me a while to work out. We just cracked on and built the business and then of course, when we sold it, there was another battleground waiting with all these men running the company who bought us.

— **And was that sale to Dentsu?**

— Yes. It was called Aegis at the time. When we came to sell, Aegis was establishing itself as a major European media network. It was buying companies across Europe, putting them together and then it went from European to global. About six years ago they sold to Dentsu, the Japanese company. We were part of that whole period of Aegis acquiring businesses and that would have been very much David's role, selling the company, making money so he could retire. He led all of that. When we were selling the company, I decided I just didn't want to work with David any more. I'd had enough. My approach seems quite naïve now but I went to see the new potential owners and I said, 'Look, I'm not coming. I just wanted you to know that. I just felt I should be straight with you.' I hadn't really thought it all through before announcing it like that and their reply was, 'If you don't come we're not buying the company.' There's no way to know for sure if that was true or not. They also said, 'We see you as the future of the business.' I remember going home and not sleeping much that night. Up until then, I'd not really asked for anything. I went in and sat down with the two partners and said, 'I've been to see the new owners and this is what I've told them and this is their response, so we have a problem. I don't want to scupper the deal for you but I don't want the current status quo to continue. This is what I want instead.' I listed a number of things and I didn't get all of them but I got most of them. That included some money because my shareholding was still quite small. I said, 'I don't want to work for the next three years as an 11% shareholder. I don't want to do the huge amount of hard work needed to hit all those targets only to get 11% of the reward. I don't feel that's fair.' That one conversation changed the way I was regarded. That was a really big lesson for me.

— **There's a lot in there about speaking up as well, just saying what you mean clearly.**

— Yes. Now I say this to young women: 'If you don't ask, you don't get.' I give them another example from much later in my career when I was awarded some share options by the CEO of Aegis. It was 40,000 share options and I was really grateful. Then I discovered a male colleague, who was less important and less effective, was given 400,000. Of course I then had a completely different feeling. The young women I speak to always say to me, 'What did you do?' I say, 'I went and talked about it and they changed the way I was rewarded. I was given a grade A which meant I got more share options, a bigger bonus and a higher salary.' So the two times I asked, I got. I think a lot of women are reluctant to ask. And I still didn't ask enough, perhaps.

— **So what was the pathway to Global President because presumably there were many, many people who could have been in that role?**

— Initially we were part of a European network. Globalisation hadn't happened. Internationalism was starting to happen. If you worked in an international role in media, it used to mean you had failed. It was just a collection of failed media directors. Then suddenly internationalism became a reality. Clients began appointing one media company across several markets. Technology was enabling this. The global CEO of Aegis said to me, 'Do you think you could create this business anywhere else in the world?' And I said, 'I've got no idea but let's have a go.' The aim was to build an international network of businesses. I had to ask in each market, 'Did something already exist here? Were there similar companies in that market? Was there something we could acquire? Or did we need to create a start-up? What was the best approach?' So, market by market, we went around the world. Nobody else was doing that so we got a first look at everything. It was a combination of acquisitions, start ups and joint ventures. I was involved right at the beginning of every business that now exists in the Posterscope network.

— **It sounds like an enormous amount of work.**

— My very first meeting was in Italy. They said, 'Why are you doing this?' I remember talking to them, explaining the idea and by the end of the meeting they said, 'Okay, we're going to do it with you.' Right from the beginning I learned the importance of influencing people by explaining the benefit to them. That made it much easier for me later on when I was working with this large matrix of separate, international businesses. Other people who have come from a position of command and control into a matrix role have really struggled. But it was different for me. Because I created the Posterscope network, I knew you had to collaborate with every single market even though the decision was going to be made centrally. I understood the importance of persuading them and working with them and gaining their trust and confidence so that I could lead them.

— **That's a different kind of power. Just the words you use demonstrate that, words like 'trust',**

'cooperate', 'lead together'.

— Yes, it's very different and it also requires you to really listen. Each of the businesses was different. You had to understand those differences and work out with the individuals where any resistance was. What were their issues? What was the best way to collaborate with them to get round those issues? If the issue was being told what to do from the centre, then you had to find a way of not appearing to be directing from the centre. That's where my track record came in useful as well. They looked at what I'd done and they could see I knew what I was talking about.

We had the Dentsu Aegis global executive dinner last week. CEO Jerry Buhlmann, who I've worked with for a very long time, gave a little speech. It wasn't what I was expecting. It was very personal. He said, 'Annie never missed a budget, ever. I've never worked with anyone before who's never missed a budget and it's all been done with such humility. She's never really asked for anything.' I was expecting the standard, 'Years of service, blah, blah, blah'. It's true I've known him a long time but, still, it was nice. And I took it as well. I accepted it.

— **That's the really important part.**

— It is.

— **Many of the women I've spoken to as part of**

this project question whether they really are powerful. I think if I'd been talking to men that wouldn't have been up for debate. That would have been taken as read. The same is true sometimes of praise. Women will say, 'Oh, but it's the team,' or 'Oh, but we got lucky.' Anything other than say, 'Yes it was me and I did really well.' I think it's because there's a gendered idea around modesty - 'nice' girls are supposed to be quiet and modest.

— It's important that you are able to recognise your contribution. There's all kinds of self-doubt along the way but I think it's very important to accept that when you are good, it was down to you. You made that decision or you had that idea. I don't think you have to be big-headed about it but I think it's important to understand it. That gives you confidence and authority.

— **What you're talking about is having and holding power based on a platform of ability and proven outcome. It's not, 'I'm a powerful figure and my title is…' It's more, 'Look what I can do. Look at what I have done. That's where my usefulness and my power comes from.'**

— It's also true that a lot of success is intuitive. I'm thinking of a recent example in Brazil. You sit down with the team and talk something through and by the time you get to the end of the meeting, you've come up with an idea of how to move things forward. I think that comes with experience. Equally, if I didn't have an idea, I'd say, 'I'm really not sure how we're going to resolve this. I need to go away and think about it.' I don't feel pressure to resolve things immediately. But I found very often that I could resolve a problem during the process of discussing it and sometimes that was quite intuitive.

— **Is it any different when men hold power now? Has it improved?**

— I don't know if it has really. There's a continuous round of revelations about sexual abuse, whether it's in Hollywood, big business or charities, and everyone says, 'This is outrageous.' But I'm thinking, 'How long will it be before we get the message that when men hold power they abuse it?' That's what they do. One way or another, they abuse that position. Whether it's sexual abuse, physical abuse, financial abuse. Eventually power seems to corrupt men. Or maybe they're corrupt before then.

— **You never know if it's corrupt men who get power or it's men who get power that go on to become corrupt.**

— It's probably both.

— Do you think women are different with power? Do you think they're less corruptible?

— It's always dangerous to generalise but I do think so. I think women probably attain power differently. I think it takes longer. They usually have to be better at what they do. That's still true. The fact that it's said a lot doesn't make it less true. For women to get promoted they do have to work twice as hard. Therefore when they get into a position of power, there's less of a sense of entitlement. I do think entitlement is one of the issues around men and power. Men think that they're entitled to rise, entitled to lead, entitled to dominate. That in turn makes them take power less seriously and they are less responsible about it. Women are more responsible about power and how they use it. They may be more thoughtful as well. I'm not saying all men are like that. But generally I think that women, because they gain power differently, they think differently about it. Also power is not something that you necessarily focus on. I've never thought, 'Gosh, I'm powerful.' Or, 'I want to have power.' Sometimes somebody would say, 'You're in quite a powerful position here.' I might interpret that as, 'I'm in quite a strong position to make this case so I'm going to make it.' I wonder if power is a word that a lot of women connect with. I don't know if they associate themselves with the word 'power' at all.

— **Since men have always held the power, it becomes almost synonymous with masculinity in a practical way. I'm really interested to find out if there is another way of seeing power which decouples it from patriarchal power. Can we pull it into a middle ground, at least, where it can be equally owned by men and women? Power can all too easily get caught up in people's subconscious bias. It can be regarded as an essentially male thing. It can be regarded as manly to have power, or to like it, or to claim it.**

— I think that's probably true. People might say, 'He's powerful.' But they might say, 'She's got a lot of authority.' Maybe they don't use the word 'power' so much with women. The fact that men have always had power must make a difference.

— **Perhaps that's where the entitlement comes from. It's justifiable if you look at history. Men have always had power so to feel entitled to have power isn't a bizarre thing for a man to do. It's quite reasonable. It doesn't make it right but it's a reasonable assumption.**

— Yes, and they had it all.

— **A lot of the women I have been speaking to have an equivocal relationship with power. When I**

say they have power they have a similar response to you, saying, 'I wouldn't really think of myself as powerful. I wouldn't think about power as this thing to acquire and love.' Wasn't it Marcus Aurelius who said something like, 'You should have the person who least wants the power in the position of power because they'll be the sanest, wisest people?'

— Why do people want to be in those positions of power? 'I want to have a position of authority and leadership so that I can make a difference.' That seems a reasonable position as opposed to, 'I want to be powerful, so that…' What? 'I can tell everybody what to do?' Or 'I can dominate?' I think you're probably right. I think men see the acquisition of power as more of an ambition than women do.

— **Power, position, material status - that very sort of thrusting language tells us something. It's already in words like 'high-powered executive'. It all sounds very masculine and competitive. It sounds to me quite sexualised as well. You have to acknowledge though that you have had power as a woman, don't you? Power has been in your hands even though you haven't sought it necessarily for its own sake.**

— Absolutely.

— **Did it ever weigh heavily on you?**

— Yes. I can remember when I was leading Posterscope. I was building the business from scratch and I was angry, I think, for the first five years.

— **Why were you angry?**

— We set the company up in a sector that was male on the whole. When I went to see people and said, 'This is the proposition. This is who we are. This is what we can do. Would you consider giving us some business?' More often than not the reply would be, 'Annie I think you could do a good job' or 'I think you could do a better job than Joe Bloggs, but I've known him for such a long time and I'm not going to change.' That blatant 'old boy network' makes you really pissed off, after a while. On the other side of the fence, there were the media owners. We were trying to create short term displays for individual advertisers. The media owners were used to selling posters long term then putting their feet up. We were disrupting all of that. We were saying, 'No, what we want to do is put something together for every single advertiser that's different and relevant to them.' We were disrupting the whole sector. The media owners were mostly men in positions of power. I remember overhearing somebody say, 'Oh, Annie Rickard - one of those girls that will be gone in 18 months.'

— Can we talk about Jane Anger? The reason I chose Jane Anger as the companion text in this volume was because you told me men put their hands up your skirt and grabbed your breasts when you were a young woman starting out. This is also the subject of Jane Anger's pamphlet. She says you've got to watch men and she's very uncompromising about offering her views and her advice. Her text was one of the first to challenge the male gaze - the idea that in a patriarchy everything is filtered through the eyes of men including the lives and the meaning and value of women. Jane Anger is arguably the first author to say, 'We're all being looked at through the eyes of men and everything we do is measured in that way and now I'm going to do it a different way as a female writer.' I thought that was really fascinating. Are you aware of your life and your business life having been subject to the male gaze?

— When you're a working mother with two small children and you're building a business, there's not much time for reflection. There's only so much you can take on. But as time passed, one of the things I realised is that businesses tend to be created by men with male rules, male criteria for success, male everything, really. Once you start to recognise that, you realise that all the judging is done by men, all the measuring is done by men. That's why I think it's quite difficult for women to succeed. It's set up for men, if you like. The whole thing is structured for male success.

— **Jane Anger repeats the idea more than once that 'men will be men'. There will be no compromise. She writes about how women need to manoeuvre around men. The text contains her advice on how to protect yourself and how you have to manoeuvre around the fact that men are irredeemable. They will not reform. I think her main point is that they are so driven by the sex impulse. Let me read you this phrase. She talks about 'the dictator' by which I think she means male genitalia. Anger may be suggesting that men's power comes from this desire to conquer and claim and hold women sexually. It's really deep and old. Society has added many layers on top of that now but underneath it all, it's that men just want to have sex with women. That's the fundamental basis of their desire for power.**

— When Jane Anger was writing, it was unthinkable that women were educated, never mind able to work. Their whole experience of men would have been domestic and/or sexual.

That would have been it. If you put Jane Anger into the 21st Century, she could just as easily be writing about gender bias in the workplace. At the end of the day, so many super powerful men get caught out around women, sex, adultery and so on. You hear about men using company money to pay off prostitutes. Why the fuck don't they use their own money? It's sex and money. If you think about the industry I've come from, the way success is measured is by how much business you can win from clients. The right leaders aren't necessarily promoted for the right reasons. The qualities of leadership are actually quite different from the qualities needed to go out and win business. So you end up with leaders who might be brilliant at winning new clients, but they're not necessarily brilliant at being managers and leaders of businesses.

 — **I read a radical feminist tract from the 1970s that suggested penetration sums up a masculine approach to the whole of life. In this world view, action is pointed and pushes forwards. The author suggested, 'You could look at sex from an alternative viewpoint. Instead of seeing it as penetration by the penis, you could regard it as enrobement by the vagina.' I suppose everything depends on what side you're looking at sex from and where you think power lies. Either one thing is going into something**

else or something else is covering and completely enfolding the one thing. The author went on to say she liked to think of sex as illustrating the way the female anatomy enfolds all. I wonder if that describes a key difference in the way men and women hold power at a deep instinctual level. Men are driven to push outwards and women can completely hold and embrace and contain.

— I've never heard anyone express it like that before.

— **You've already talked about working around a problem and finding a way to bring everybody together. You've talked about not telling people what to do but working to bring people to concensus. Pushing outwards is very specific and it has a lot of drama in it but it strikes me as a weaker power than the ability to enfold and contain everything. That is not such an obvious 'spiked' power. It's a much more systemic power. I think a lot of what you've said today about your own experiences of leading are about bringing everyone into a place, not just prodding at people to make them do things. It's an enfolding kind of power.**

— But equally, when you're building a business, you have to take tough decisions sometimes. I think it's important to take those tough decisions and to be seen to be taking them. If that means removing people from senior positions, you have to do that. When the business was my own, I used to think about the best way forward so that it could grow. When it belonged to the shareholders, I used to think about what's right for them. You have to be able to take those tough decisions. Equally, in that matrix of international businesses, where you're collaborating and influencing and so on, there are moments where you have to ruffle some feathers. You can't achieve everything through influence. You're going to have to say, 'We need to have a conversation about this. This is what I think you've got to do in order to take this forward.' You've got to get tough about it. You have to know when to strike. You have to be really clear. What do you want the outcome to be? What's the downside of making that move on that individual? What's the worst that can happen? I've done that in the matrix and come out the other side in a positive way. My status within the group at that time would have helped.

— **How do you feel about confrontation?**

— If it's specific to a business issue, I never minded it.

— **Do you get nervous about it?**

— I would get anxious about it but I would do my homework. I would think through what I'm going to do and say. What they might say in return and my response. I would be suitably nervous, but not frightened. On a personal level, having a row with somebody, I don't like it at all. Not at all. But I can do it in business. Going back to the sex thing, what's quite funny is where you get financial irregularities, there's always a bit of sex involved as well. Someone might be cheating on the company but they are also charging for all these prostitutes on the company as well. Their expenses are full of all of this stuff. They usually go hand in hand. There's rarely one without the other which I think is interesting. And that is Jane Anger's point. She's right. I'm trying to think of all the cases where we have exited somebody and it's been reasonably senior and dramatic in that sense and they've usually involved expenses receipts as well… from clubs.

— **Jane Anger says, because of sex, you can't trust any man. No man is trustworthy.**

— I agree, I'm sorry to say. An awful lot of men would cry out in horror and say, 'Annie, that's simply not true.' But I think it might be, actually. The aim is to get the girl and have the sex.

— **Anger also says, once they've had you, then they are awful and they just complain all the time. Before they've had you, it's all about how marvellous you are and your virtues are limitless. She does also**

say that not all women are marvellous either and she cites a lot of women in classical mythology who have cheated their husbands and run off with lovers. Helen of Troy keeps turning up. Not all women are marvellous and gentle and not all men are terrible and corrupt.

— Women make up 50% of the population and within that you're going to get some really bright women and some really stupid women, some greedy women and some scheming women. That's true because that's humanity. There will, of course, be women who scheme and women who abuse power. Everyone's keen to find examples of women who are bullies when they get into positions of seniority. I've heard people say publicly, 'The problem with women, of course, is when they do get to these positions, they are so awful to other women.' Is that true? Are they really as bad to other women as men have been for all these years? I doubt it. It may be that they are just not overtly helping other women and maybe they are just telling it how it is to women who are not very good at their jobs. Or maybe they are just unpleasant women. I went to a wine tasting in a club in Pall Mall. One of the women there had been the first female something or other in the City. She said, 'My daughter's always talking about feminism and I take the view that I've done my bit for women.' And I thought, 'You haven't done anything for women, you just happen to have been the first female such and such.' It's not a case of 'all men are bad, all women are good'. We're the same, that's the whole point. We are equal and we are the same. But within that, I do think it's fair to say that men have a different attitude to sex in the main. Not all men and not all women but in the main, they do see it differently. They do see it as a conquest. There are those examples in history, in real life, everywhere. Once they've achieved the conquest, they move on. I think it's true.

— **Jane Anger gives some great advice at the end of her essay. She says, 'Think well of as many men as you want to. Love the ones you have reason to love. Hear everything they say. Hate all those who speak against women or dishonour the female sex.'**

— What prompted her to write her pamphlet?

— **She was writing in response to another pamphlet called *Book his Surfeit in Love*. It was about an 'over-indulging lover', a man who had gorged on sex and therefore was jaded with it. It was a big success, very insulting towards women, and it made her angry. It's seen as unfeminine to give in to anger. Whereas when men give in to anger, it's not necessarily a good thing, but it's very masculine.**

— If you were to go into a room of a hundred women in business and say, 'Hands up everybody who's been accused of being emotional at work,' I think the whole hundred women would put their hands up. Emotion is not a gendered thing. It's a human reaction. Men have made emotion gendered and negative. They say things like, 'Don't be so emotional, dear.' Whereas emotion is an incredibly useful tool when you're a manager and a leader, if used well. It is also a natural human instinct or characteristic. But it has become gendered.

— **It's also implied that there's a correlation between being emotional and weakness. Yet neuroscience tells us we make decisions emotionally first and then the rational decision follows a few nanoseconds later. The rational decision is a post-rationalisation of the first emotional response. The idea of 'rational thought' is a myth.**

— Emotion is a powerful and important characteristic. To have it made negative in that way, and gendered, is outrageous really. That's another thing I say when giving a talk to young women, 'Next time your boss or a guy in the office tells you to stop being so emotional, just say to yourself quietly, 'Emotion is not a gendered thing.''

— **Do women tend to be more emotionally**

intelligent? It may not be innate. It may be because they've been allowed to develop that skill as youngsters, whereas 'big boys don't cry'. Because it becomes a skill associated with women, the patriarchy makes it a negative thing.

— Possibly, yes.

— **As I look at these questions around power, you see a lot of things are dismissed by the patriarchy when it's men that don't tend to be good at them.**

— Because they don't think about or don't understand it, it doesn't have any value. They think, 'I don't even know what that is and I'm a powerful man. I don't care.' I get quite angry when I'm talking about these things and reading about them and thinking about them.

— **I wonder why women aren't more angry. Why do women put up with such a lot? I suppose until very recently women couldn't even own property and if a man beat his wife up, he was just being a good husband keeping her in check. The fear of either starvation and poverty or physical violence has probably, for the majority of the time, been women's lived experience. Perhaps women can't afford to be angry because they'll be homeless or black and blue.**

— That's still true today for a lot of women.

— **If women can't take part in independent economic activity, they are vulnerable.**

— I remember early on somebody saying to me, 'Oh, are you one of those career women?' I'm going back here almost to the beginning of my career and my response to that was, 'Well, I feel responsible for putting a roof over my head, so if that makes me a career woman then, yes.' I thought, 'What am I supposed to think, I don't need to worry about putting a roof over my head because a man will do that for me?' That idea seemed to me so alien. I've felt like that since the age of fifteen, sixteen. That's one thing that has been consistent. And it could be one of the things that drove me to do all that work. At the heart of it all was the desire to be independent.

— **How would you describe male power?**

— Probably quite negatively. I would say that it's the ability to take control, make decisions and dominate. Those are the sort of words I'd use.

— **How would you describe female power?**

— Hard-earned, and I would imagine therefore more thoughtful. One of the toughest things I had to do was let a long-standing colleague go. His reaction was one of anger and it stayed like that. The reason he was angry with me was because he felt that I had taken something off him that was his. It was his job and his career and I had ruined it. He couldn't look beyond the idea that I ruined it for him. I think that's because he had a massive sense of entitlement. This is my job and she's spoilt it and taken it off me.

— **It's interesting isn't it because women are constantly having things taken off them but they don't get so angry.**

— The first thing a woman says is: 'Was it me?'

— **Is that a weakness or a strength?**

— I think probably both, but on balance, it might be a weakness.

JANE ANGER

Jane Anger was a 16th-century English author. She was the first woman to publish a full-length defence of the female sex in English.

In the late 16th Century, it was unusual for women to write and publish on non-religious themes. It was also rare for a woman to argue against male supremacy.

Her pamphlet *Jane Anger, Her Protection for Women* (1589) is an early feminist rejection of negative portrayals of women's character and intellectual capacity.

Jane Anger's work responds to a misogynistic pamphlet, probably the anonymous (and now lost) *Book his Surfeit in Love*. The book was printed by Thomas Orwin and may well have been authored by Orwin himself.

Book his Surfeit in Love consisted of mocking broadsides on the nature of womanhood. Jane Anger refers to the authorial voice in Orwin's pamphlet as 'the surfeiting lover', rendered in this modern English version as 'the over-indulging lover'. Her writing blends witty invective with shrewd and well-observed psychological insights into the nature of the tensions between the sexes.

Scholars know virtually nothing more about Jane Anger's life. She is known only by her name, which may have been a pseudonym.

JANE ANGER'S PROTECTION FOR WOMEN

To defend them against the scandalous reports of an over-indulging lover,[2] and all other similar fools who complain of being gorged on sex.

Dear Women of England,

There is always the risk that, in your level-headedness, you'll reject this text because I wrote it out of anger. Maybe Jane Anger will provoke your anger. You might prefer not to be associated with someone as full of rage as I am. But please wait before you judge me. Take the side of the defendant, not the prosecutor. I'm afraid you'll pass judgment before the trial has even begun - which is against the law - although my hot-headedness may well deserve it.

I won't say to you, 'Come on, be reasonable!' because you are intelligent and you'll soon see that the points I'm trying to make are all too reasonable. I won't write too much for fear of becoming long-winded and annoying. And I'll try to write as clearly as possible so no one can accuse me of being deliberately over-clever or obscure. Forgive me if I come across as arrogant but I wrote in a fit of anger. I've put down my ideas about how you can protect yourselves from unscrupulous men. As a writer, I now put myself in your hands. You be the judge of the results.

Yours, Jane Anger

To all women in general, and to the reader, whoever you may be: damn the falsehood of men whose imaginations are feverishly overactive. As soon as they start speaking, they start hurling insults. Was anyone ever so abused, slandered, insulted, or unfairly treated as we women? Are the gods going to allow this to go on? Are the goddesses going to hold back from punishing injustice? Are we, ourselves, going to demand that men are held to account for their wickedness? The church stands idly by when men who abuse women should be hanged! Let the London sewers overflow so violently that men are flushed out from their safe houses. Let the pavements be icy and the soles of men's shoes as smooth as glass. Let the streets be as steep as the slopes of Mount Etna and every gust of wind like an icy whirlwind blown out of the throat of Boreas, god of winter.[3] All to ensure that these men go to hell as quickly as possible. Over-indulging lovers have the audacity to complain about receiving too much of women's kindness. Are you women going to just stand there and say nothing? Am I, Jane Anger, going to use every bit of my ingenuity and my abilities as a writer to challenge their gorging on sex? Yes I am! And I ask you to support me so that I can be of use to the cause of women. Take care.

Your friend,

Jane Anger.

Protection for Women

It seems every man wants to reveal his true nature by writing about it. It's laughable. They're all style and no content. They get so carried away, trying to write impressively, that they lose track of their own arguments and their writing ends up all over the place. When they've exhausted all their other ideas, the only thing they can think of is to write about women. If they can get just close enough to glimpse the edge of a petticoat, they think the god Apollo[4] has blessed them with an infinite supply of women to soothe the headaches they've given themselves trying to think of new ways to criticise us. They want God to see how thankful they are for sending them women. But their senses are so inflamed and their minds are so crazed with desire that they immediately start criticising and slandering our 'silly' sex. What is the cause of this hatred towards women? Without a doubt it is the so-called 'weakness of our intellects', and because men think we're too timid to challenge their lies and insults. Their lying tongues are so short, they think we can't catch hold of them and pull them out. They've been bandying about their criticisms of women for so long, they think we'll never put pen to paper to retaliate. This has made them cocky and, unless we put the fear of God into them, they'll think they've won. They have been so well looked after, out of the kindness of our hearts, that they're like weary mares whose stomachs have become queasy - now they're simply sick of women's kindness. If we don't let them sniff at our underwear, they grab our petticoats. If we don't put up with their groping, they'll say we're prudes, but if we play along with them, even a little, they'll immediately make a huge fuss, going on about how they've 'had it up to here' with love. All the time trying to show how clever and witty they are in the process.

Men have done just that in countless books recently. Without even having to look for it, *Book his Surfeit in Love*, (the complaining of an old lover, gorged on sex, circulated to protect other men from a similar fate) came to me by chance. I glanced over it because women enjoy interesting reading just as much as men. I liked the ending of the book just as much as the beginning. I was so carried away by the imagination of the writer that I had finished the book before I knew it - his sentences were so precise, his diction was so clear, his style was so elegant. The book contained two main arguments: one blaming men's own stupidity, and the other insulting women. Men's stupidity is the result of their ludicrous self-promotion, according to the writer, whereas women's foolishness comes simply from being women, which has some truth in it!

The long passage about the lust-filled King Ninus[5] can

be summed up like this: he over-indulged in sex simply because every time he asked for it, he got it. How men flatter themselves! They know we women are frail. We are easily overwhelmed. Power bends everything to itself. Men take King Ninus as their inspiration and justify overpowering women who are so much weaker. If we resist, they try harder. If we show any sign of weakness, they'll keep going until they've conquered us. Semeramis[6] left her husband for King Ninus and who wouldn't when his flattery was so incessant? In the end, Ninus gave his life for his kingdom and was a fool to have done so. And this is my criticism of him (I agree with the over-indulging lover in *Book his Surfeit in Love*, except that he has put some of the wrong words in the wrong places.)

Fools force such flattery, and men of dull wits:
But such frenzy often also haunts the wise (once Nurse Wisdom
*   has been rejected)*
Though love be sure and firm: yet lust fraught with deceit,
And men's fair words bring about great pain, unless they
*   are suspected.*
Then foolish Ninus had what was coming to him,
*   if I his judge might be,*
Wild are men's lusts, false are the lips, filthy with flattery.
Himself and his kingship - which surpassed all - he enslaved,

His foot-stool he made his pillow and therefore was a beast.
I wish the Gods to send beastly ends to all such beasts,
And if there's a worse end, I wish him to send that too
And so, my censure ends.

The terrible deeds of the lazy king Sardanapalus[7] - and his well-deserved sticky end - are so clearly and honestly laid out in *Book his Surfeit in Love*, that I have to agree with the author.

But his praise of Menelaus,[8] the husband of Helen of Troy, is unbelievable. Men are so like bulls, it's no wonder that the gods transform some of them into actual bulls as a warning to the rest - assuming they take it that way. Some of them chase after women just as a bull chases after a cow. But in case they trip and crack open their skulls, the gods put a pair of horns on their heads to prevent them from hitting the ground.[9] That was the case with Menelaus, for sure. He went gallivanting about sniffing women's underwear and he ended up a cuckold. This is my verdict of him:

The most-just Gods do justly punish sin
With those same plagues which make men most forlorn.
If filthy lust starts to spring in men
For that monstrous sin they are plagued by the horns.

The Gods very wisely forewarn men,
To shun wild lust, otherwise they too will wear the horns.
Deceitful men must be repaid with guile
And a blow for a blow gives way to another blow.
The man who is afraid of the cuckold's fate,
Ought to refrain from lechery
Otherwise he'll have the plague he so fears,
And will end up having to wear the horns.
The Greek wore Actaeon's badge,[10] they say
And worthy of it too, because he loved the smock so much,
I pray that every lusty man may be a bull,
That way, poor women shall have peace
Thus does my censure cease.

The greatest fault women have is that we are so ready to believe the things men say. If we could flatter men as much as they lie to us, and use our intelligence for our own good as much as they use their tongues for mischief, none of them would ever complain of having too much sex. If women are as treacherous as they say, it's a wonder that the gods made the figure of Fidelity[11] a woman and not a man. The gods knew that there was some fine quality in women which is not in men. But before some man can catch me as I trip up, (telling me I'm stupid or mad because it's so obvious that men are superior to women, and women ought to obey men), I answer back as follows: the gods knew that men are always ambitious. They looked at women's many wonderful qualities and wanted to prevent us from becoming vain. So they decided to let men be superior. Now men are left with only this flimsy claim to boast about, and for God's sake, let them keep it... But let's return to *Book his Surfeit in Love*.

Having discussed at length the gods' disapproval of love, the author leaves the gods (and so do I) and turns to the principal object and foundation of love, which he declares to be woman. Now referring to the text of his pamphlet, in which there are many taunts against women, he says that we deliberately lure men to us. He's closer to the truth than he realises because we do attract men with our best qualities, and they marry us just to make themselves look good. Men are clever enough to recognise our value. They are delighted by our femininity, which appeals to their senses. They then behave like ravenous hawks who don't just want to possess us, they want to devour us. Our love for men is self-destructive. Women are beautifully put together, only to be horribly messed up by men. Men make a mockery of our good natures, rewarding our love with patronising disrespect. It makes sense to call women 'the grief of man' in that women really do take grief from men. We're neglected while they laugh. We lie sighing when they sit singing. We sit sobbing while they lie lazily asleep. Mulier est in hominis confusio (woman is man's confusion) because she's too kind to confront him as forcefully as he deserves. She either loves or hates. There's no in-between. She loves good things and hates everything bad. She loves justice and hates wrongdoing. She loves truth and truthfulness and hates lies and dishonesty. She loves man for his good qualities and hates him for his faults. In short, there is no middle ground between good and bad and no woman ever sits on the fence.

A complete fool once asked Plato whether women should be regarded as reasonable or unreasonable. Plato's answer revealed the beauty of his mind as well as any of his books. He knew that women are the greatest allies men have. Men can't live without the help of women any more than they can live without meat, drink, clothing or other necessities. In his own time, Plato knew that men had become unreasonable and were likely to become more so as time went on. Men were so unreasonable that he couldn't decide whether it was men or brute beasts that had the least reason. Unless a woman is as beautiful as Venus, men can't stand the sight of her. Their stomachs are so sickly that if they taste the same dish twice, they've had too much of it and a new dish must be found for them. We are the opposite of men because they are the opposite of goodness. They are blind as bats so they cannot see our true natures but we can see theirs only too well, even if we're only half looking. That's how bad they are. We have to watch what we're doing every day because men's redeeming qualities become less by the hour.

If only the Greek poet Hesiod[12] had examined the life of man as precisely as he examined the qualities of woman. Then he would have said that a woman who trusts a man is like someone with a 1000lb weight around her neck dropped into a bottomless sea. We are confused by men and sometimes they are annoyed by us. We criticise them because we genuinely disapprove of their filthy vices. They view our good advice as nagging because it doesn't support their foolish ideas. They see our bravery as rash when we answer them back. They think we're disobedient if we don't agree with their mad ideas. They call our anger dangerous simply because we won't put up with their foolish behaviour.

If our frowns are that terrible and our anger is that deadly, then men are mad for provoking us. If they didn't cross us, a terrible death could be prevented! There is eternal hatred between the wild boar and the tame hounds. I think that there should be the same tension between women and men, unless men change their ways. Then strength would be their chief characteristic rather than flattery and dishonesty as now. The lion rages when he is hungry but men rage when they are full. The tiger is robbed of her cubs when she wanders far off, but men steal women's virginity from right under their noses. The viper attacks when his tail is trodden on, but a woman is not allowed to protest when her body is used as little more than a prop for men's desire. Their unreasonable minds have no idea what reason is, which makes them little better than brute beasts.

Clytemnestra,[13] Ariadne,[14] Delilah[15] and Jezebel[16] were all accused of having loose morals. Shouldn't Nero[17] be added to that list, along with others too many to name? It's a sad fact that Deianira[18] was falsely accused of her husband Hercules' death. She was utterly blameless of any crime (even in her thoughts). If the centaur's lies hadn't fooled her, Hercules wouldn't have died, cruelly tormented, and the centaur's deception wouldn't have worked so unfortunately well. But we are expected to put up with these mistakes, and even worse ones in *Book his Surfeit in Love*, because the writer had been sent half mad by too much sex. In spite of his own arguments he missed the whole point: instead of falsely accusing Deianira, he should have condemned Hercules.

Marius'[19] daughter had so many excellent qualities, she was too good for Metellus[20] or any other man living. She may not have been perfect, but Metellus was infinitely worse, committing numerous terrible crimes. Where feathers grow on the hen's head, a coxcomb grows on the cockerel's. Women may annoy men, but men bring women worry, poverty, grief and constant fear, all of which are far worse.

Euthydemus[21] classified women into six types. I suggest there are as many types of men: rich, poor, bad, good, foul and fair. The inheritances wealthy men leave their children make those children rich. Gambling and other misfortunes turn them into poor beggars. Gluttons kept on a strict diet stay healthy but if they're allowed to eat what they like, they gorge themselves and become good-for-nothing. There are gorgeous men whose faces are as fine as porcelain. But when I say 'fair men', I'm not referring to men like these. I mean men who are fair in the sense of not being unreasonable. When I say 'foul men', I mean men that are not polite or honest. None of these men is any good. None of them is rich or handsome for long. If we want men to be good, we have to prevent them from over-indulging themselves. Otherwise they'll overdo it every time. In other words, wealth makes them spend, spend, spend, wit makes them foolish, beauty makes them vain, poverty makes them deceitful and deformity makes them ugly. So heed my warning:

Think of men as you would a broken reed,
Never trust them, and you shall succeed.

If this is true (and it's difficult to see how it can be otherwise), isn't it also true that a goose in front of a ravenous fox is just like a woman who trusts a man's loyalty? The goose stands to lose its head, the woman is guaranteed to lose her reputation if there's the slightest whiff of suspicion. The fellow who thought his wife was a terrible nag is a fool and will always be a fool. His true loyalty was to his pot of ale. His wife tried to stop him drinking and he was so blinded by rage that he didn't know what he was doing.

When food is in short supply, a fat man will feel it most, but a slim man will hardly notice it all. The dictator's son was in pain as long as his cock was crowing, but dealing with the craving, he made his master hang down his head.[22]

Thales[23] was so randy that he didn't give a damn if a woman was married or not. Most men will do something in the heat of the moment, and regret it later, but he was completely immoral. Like men today, he couldn't bear to hear women praised or men criticised. It's best if men like this follow King Alfonso's[24] rule: make themselves deaf and marry blind wives. That way they'll never have to hear their wives praised and their wives will never have to see their husbands' womanising.

When the poet Tibullus[25] made up rules for women to follow, he could have spared a thought for men too. He might have said, 'Every honest man should avoid anything that puts his health or safety at risk, and he should try not to lie or shout insults. He must be modest and show his modesty through good and civilised behaviour. He should be careful not to show how crude he is by using filthy words. Lying lips and deceitful tongues are abominable before God.' It's easy to convince a cat to catch a mouse, and even easier to persuade a desperate man to kill himself. There's no changing the nature of the things. As the over-indulging lover said in his pamphlet, what's bred in the bone will come out in the flesh. If we wear sacks and tie up our hair in dishcloths, men will still chase us. If we want to cover ourselves up, only leather will do - no cloth can keep a man's hands off our breasts.

We roll our eyes and they complain all the time. Our eyes make them look at us lustily. Why? Because they are naturally sex mad. It's easy to find a stick to beat a dog, and a burnt finger quickly teaches someone to be careful of the fire. If men would only take advice as well as they give it out, Socrates' rule[26] would be better followed. Socrates, heaven and earth can say what they like - a man's face is as steady and trustworthy as a reflection rippling in a glass of water. I'll finish with a proverb - however much you write, you'll never describe the full extent of man's dishonesty. I wish the ancient writers had spent as much time describing men's faults as they did outlining the foolishness of women. I wish someone would question that bias which still remains unchallenged. But since all their energy has been used up maintaining that biased view of the world, I leave them to get on with it and return to the over-indulging lover as he returns to his discussion of love.

Now that the greedy glutton is busy with his theory on love (which has no bearing on the subject in hand) let's consider, in secret and amongst ourselves, how our worst enemies - men - are both inferior to us and dependent on our kindness.

When man and woman were first created, man was made out of dross and filthy clay. God saw that his handiwork work was good, and that the transformation of dirt into flesh had made it pure. Next God considered a companion for man and created woman out of man's flesh, which proves that she was purer still, and women are better than men. Women are able to have children and contribute to the population of the earth. A woman's care and concern is a wonderful thing and keeps men safe. Man's salvation, Jesus Christ, was born from a woman. The first Christian believer was a woman and a woman was the first to ask forgiveness for her sins. Only women can be truly loyal, and without women there is no homemaking. When men are ill, we're indispensable to them, and when they're healthy, they can't do without us. We make them comfortable and prepare their meals for them. We keep them clean for the sake of their health, which would suffer otherwise because of poor hygiene. Without our care they would lie in bed like a litter of dogs, and stink like mackerel in the heat of summer. They love to look their best and take pride in their appearance but they can only do it because we make sure everything about them is well put together. Our virginity reflects our good moral character, our nature makes us polite and our chastity ensures our honesty about our love lives is self-evident.[27] Men say we're a necessary evil. Men couldn't do without us, that's true, but I object to the idea that women are evil, except, perhaps, in relation to men. Men hate all good things and only desire bad things, and consequently their desire for us makes us bad, according to them. If anyone contradicted me saying that only God is good, and therefore all women are evil, I'd have to agree with them. But men are no better, given that they can't do without us. If we are evil, they are certainly worse - evil on top of evil makes a worse evil. People who make use of evil are worse than evil. If men are going to contradict the Magnificat,[28] they must first learn the meaning of it. Men cannot deny that we are generous since many of them have, by their own admission, received more kindness from us in one day than they can repay in a whole year. Some have gorged on sex with us to such an extent that they cry 'No more!' If men claim women are fools, we can prove them wrong. I, myself, have heard men say that we are too clever for our own good, so how can we possibly be fools? Some men are less wise than they should be, and therefore fools. According to some men, all a woman needs to know is how to avoid a shower of rain and find her way to her husband's bed. But this is 1588. These days, men have become so unrealistic and impractical that unless we show how foolish they are, we'll just look foolish ourselves. And now (given that I am only speaking to women) I'll prove that a woman's wisdom is superior to a man's. And I'll do it in a scholarly way but without complicated or unnecessarily clever arguments. Wisdom comes only from grace. This is a principle. And no one can dispute matters of principle. Grace was first given to a woman, the Virgin Mary, so we can conclude that women are wise. Now, 'first is best' as the truism goes, so women must be wiser than men. We are naturally cleverer than men. This is easily proved by the fact that men are often confused by our arguments, and if they're talking about worldly things, they must take our advice or be proven fools in the end.

By chance, I heard a story about two wise men (German

cousins from the town of Gotha) who made complete asses of themselves. A ring was stolen from one of the men's rooms. He was so incensed about the theft that he couldn't sleep. He went to ask for his friend's advice about recovering the stolen property. His friend was shocked by the sight of him, with his clothes all dishevelled. The friend assumed the man must be laid low by something like a migraine so he offered him a handkerchief to wrap around his head. The man was suddenly incensed, complaining that his friend had got it all wrong. He started to rant and rave, cursing the day he was born and the Fates for allowing him to live. His friend misjudged the situation again, thinking that the man was now possessed by some kind of demon. He turned to run but was stopped by the man who told him he was mistaken again. Seeing that the man was very disturbed, and realising that he couldn't get away from him, the friend pulled himself together and asked him what was really the matter. The man sat down and explained it was the theft of the ring, which had been stolen from his window. He asked if he should go to a Wise Woman to find out what had happened to it. His friend agreed and asked whether the man knew any Wise Women. Between them they knew a great many, and together went in search of one, which is where we shall leave them.

Now tell me whether or not you think these men were

wise. In particular, didn't they demonstrate wisdom by their actions? They hoped to find what had been lost through the foolishness of a man with the help of the wisdom of a woman! According to an old proverb, 'the wisdom of a woman is a great matter: let men learn to be wiser or give themselves away as fools'. By turning to a Wise Woman for help, the men clearly realised that women are no fools.

Now the over-indulging lover leaves his theorising on love and returns to insulting women. Let's be patient and look more closely at what he's saying so we can understand his over-indulging a little better. His book was printed so recently it would be unfair to the publisher to repeat too much of the text here. So I'll simply refer you to *Book his Surfeit in Love*, and come to my point. To enjoy a woman is like catching the devil by the foot. To enjoy a man is like holding the devil tightly around his middle. In the first case the devil can easily break free but in the second he cannot escape unless he takes the man with him.

In nature, the snake stings and the eel is slippery. But men's tongues sting against nature all the time and are therefore basically unnatural. Suppose we put up with men as much as possible and give into them even when it's not convenient. By the end of a year, we'll have lost more than they have gained, and they'll have gained immeasurably. In nature, the chameleon can change his colour but a man always stays the same - stuck with his own dishonesty and unreliability. The sting of the scorpion is cured by the scorpion, so the scorpion must have some good in its nature. But men don't stop telling stinging lies until honesty is dead. Gloves take the risk out of picking roses and a bee-keeper's hood makes handling bees safe. But nothing can take the risk out of a man's dishonesty and unreliability.

If men are mad enough to battle against nature itself, it's not surprising if nature gives them a good run for their money. If Tom Fool[29] wants to ride Alexander's horse,[30] no one should feel sorry for him if he gets a nasty kick. But it seems that the author of *Book his Surfeit in Love* has had a great deal of experience of Italian courtesans, which accounts for his wisdom in the question of love. Life imitates art: and someone who has experience to prove his point is in a better position than someone who has to rely on book learning alone.

A man's smooth talking is like a cloud gliding from place to place until it fills up with rain and spits out a terrible shower. Men flatter women until they get what they want, and then they come raining down on us even though we never did anything to hurt them. It's sensible to be on your guard for snakes hidden in the grass. But when the snake lies out in the open in autum and winter, its bite is all the more painful because it is so unexpected. Be suspicious when men say they'll keep something secret because they're bound to be up to something. A dirty old man always disguises himself in a monk's robes.

It's amazing how men flatter themselves. If a woman so much as looks at them, they'll jump straight to the conclusion that she fancies them. If they're feeling randy, they'll say she has fallen in love them. Just the idea of having a woman is enough to make them want half a dozen in one night - and they swear they'll die if they don't get them. It's no wonder they over-indulge themselves when they're so greedy for sex. But wouldn't it be worse if any of these men died (because they're so easily killed by a lack of sex)? Better to be safe than sorry. If we manage to get away from them, they'll say they've had us anyway. Some of them are so shameless, they'll boast to their friends that they've slept with a woman when they've only spoken to her once, if that. You must bear with them because they're not in the habit of lying! They'll say, 'We're not liars!' But you're as likely to hear the truth come out of their mouths as you are to see wild geese fly under London Bridge. Their displays of affection are nothing but flattery. Their promises to be faithful are lies. Their compliments lure women into having sex with them. They promise the earth, but what they bring is death, or an evil worse than death. Their singing is bait to catch us, their playing is a plague to torment us. So beware of them, and take this advice as a wise precaution and a legal rule-of-thumb: never, ever, trust men. There are three aspects to men, which are inextricable: lust, deceit and spite. They use flattery to get what's in their filthy minds, and they use their writing to spread their nasty ideas. A little bile sours anything sweet and a lying tongue spoils all the other good parts of a man.

Didn't Vulcan's stupidity in wooing Briceris encourage Venus to deceive him in turn?[31] Wasn't it Paris' flattery that tempted Helen to betray her husband?[32] Without doubt. And when the over-indulging lover says he doesn't want his writing to come across as unreasonable, it's just flannel - instead of blaming his writing, he should be blaming his randiness. The love of Hipsicrates[33] and Panthea,[34] the dedication of Artemesia[35] and Portia,[36] the affection of Sulpitia[37] and Aria,[38] the true love of Hipparchia[39] and Piscae,[40] the loving passions of Macrina[41] and the wife of Pandoerus[42] - they all appear in *Book his Surfeit in Love*. They reveal how indiscreet men's minds are and the way men's hearts revel in nothing but mischief. There's no point crying over spilt milk. Why then should Sigismundus[43] be discussed at such length? Her husband was dead and consequently she was free to associate with any man she liked. The tongue says out loud what lies in the heart. This is clear to see when men write complaining texts like *Book his Surfeit in Love*. Of all immoral pleasures, they say womanising is the greatest and yet some men are not ashamed to confess publicly that they have over-indulged in it. It degrades the body, it makes it stink and yet men still do it. It's a wonder women can stand men at all. Perhaps it's only because they deceive us into putting up with them, in much the same way as we are supposed to deceive them with perfumes.

Immoral pleasure is a strong beast, and has many ways of making men feel desire. But men are so enthusiastic anyway, they don't really need any encouragement. Lord Lust's courtyard is already so full of men that he needs to make stronger gates to keep them out, rather than throwing them open to let men in. But if he did try to keep men out he'd be lynched by the crowd. If men would only follow the examples of abstinent King Cyrus,[44] Zenocrates,[45] Caius Gracchus,[46] Pompeius[47] and Francis Duke of Millaine[48] (all of whom appear in *Book his Surfeit in Love*). There'd be no over-indulging in sex then. I pray to God that men will mend their ways. But in the meantime, they need to bear in mind that reckless behaviour calls for forgiveness. Lying hearts meet tragic ends. Flattery leads to all kinds of foolishness, and a lying tongue is simply the mouthpiece of a lying heart.

I've described the way men trick women, not so you'll condemn all men, but so that you'll be aware of their innate dishonesty and ignore their flattery. It is reasonable that the hens who lay the eggs and hatch the chicks should be fed first. But by the same token, it's unreasonable that the cocks who mate with them should go unfed. There are brave and true men. And honourable men who cannot bear deception. There are some men who are incapable of wholehearted love and many who are constantly randy. There are men who are worthwhile, but the majority don't care how many lies they have to tell to get a woman into bed. They are like Envy who would be happy to lose one eye if it meant someone else would have to lose both eyes. Think well of as many men as you can. Love them when there's a good reason to. Hear everything they say (shaking your head when they make fools of themselves) but believe very little, if any, of it. And reject all men who say anything to denigrate women.

Let the luxurious life of Heliogabalus,[49] the excessive desires of Commodus[50] and Proculus,[51] the terrible lusts of Chilpericus[52] and Xerxes,[53] the violent rapes of Boleslaus,[54] and the unnatural carnal appetite of Sigismundus Malotesta[55] be enough to persuade you that what men really want is filthy and immoral sex. The Romans and other wise lawmakers passed sound legislation but none of it is enough to stop men from feeling sexual desire. In England, men who commit crimes against women face terrible punishment but that doesn't stop them from committing them anyway.

The over-indulging lover's advice is good, if only he and his companions would follow it. But when the fox starts preaching, the geese need to beware because there's about to be a massacre. It isn't cheating to trick a tricker, and it's not a sin to slaughter an animal whose only instinct is to kill. If you want to please men, you must follow their lead, and flatter them shamelessly - men and the honest truth are strangers. A thing is more precious if it's hard won. Something that costs the most should be the best. Crowns are expensive and something that costs many crowns must be worth it, please God, otherwise you've worked hard and spent money for nothing. If any man gives such good advice as the over-indulging lover, you'd be a fool to refuse it. I know you want to know what that advice is, bought at such high a price. So here goes - the over-indulging lover's text and my comments on it will reveal it now.

At the end of men's promises is a trap. From now on, don't listen when men claim to be your friends otherwise they'll ruin you before you know it. The path that leads to the trap is man's deceitfulness. Trees act as milestones along the path and those trees are called Folly, Vice, Mischief, Lust, Deceit and Pride but they are disguised as Imagination, Virtue, Modesty, Love, Truth and Handsomeness. Folly will welcome you. It will tell you what you stand to gain by coming this way then direct you towards Vice who is even craftier. He will praise you lavishly, listing all the ways men are indebted to women: but once our backs are turned, he hurls insults instead. Then Mischief looks us carefully up and down to see if there is any cranny he can get his finger into and widen it far enough to fit in his tongue. Now we come to Lust. He will lecture against flirting and ban womanising, saying 'to the devil with it!' - but he never means it. Deceit will give you compliments while picking your pockets and he'll steal your heart, if you're not careful! But when you hear a man objecting to fine textiles, embroidery, periwigs, the clothing of courtesans and the pride of all women in general, know he's a wolf in sheep's clothing and you're standing on the shores of your own destruction. So protect yourselves from men, which you can do by ignoring their flattery - a man's flattery is the forerunner of a woman's ruin. If an old horse is lame, he'll wince when he walks. And you can't blame a young horse for rearing up when the spurs are used on him. The old horse will stand quietly once his lameness has healed, and the young horse will behave when he stops smarting from the spurs' jabs. Give the over-indulging lover the benefit of the doubt because he was angry when he wrote his book. Perhaps he'll regret insulting women when he's calmed down. Perhaps he'll even make a public retraction. The faltering language towards the end of his book suggests he already half-regretted writing it because his anger has passed. But don't believe him whatever he swears is the truth. An old horse may rest easy in the stable when he's no longer lame, but he'll only reveal his true nature when he's gallivanting out and about. Man's flattery gets you when you least expect it. I pray that God will keep you safe from it (and me, too).

Amen.
The End.

A sovereign salve to cure the over-indulging lover[56]

If once the heat did before thee beat
Of foolish love so blind:
Sometimes to sweat, sometimes to fret
As one out of their mind.
If wits were taken, in such a break
That reason was exiled.
And woe woke up, with no help of healing
Then love has thee, beguiled.
If anyone into your sight
Beyond all others did excel,
Whose beauty bright constrained right
Your heart with her to dwell:
If so your foe oppressed you so
That you could not go back,
But still with woe did surfeit
And this pain was thankless.
If nothing but pain remains in love,
Then let this be my advice to you:
Avoid this dangerous pain and
Do not come near it.
And once this blast has gone and past,
It would certainly be better
To fast from flesh, whilst you are alive,

Then to surfeit so again.
Learn by living,
J.A.

And likewise to the reader, from the author
Though sharp is the seed sown by Anger,
We all (almost) confess
And hard is the fate of those
Possessed by Anger,
Yet it would be hapless for the reader to reap
Such fruit from Anger's soil.
So as you please and Anger ease
From long and weary toil.
I took pain on your behalf
To till that cloddy ground
Where there was scarcely a place free from disgrace
Nor another woman to be found.
If anything I have said offends you
Put it down to my mood.
For that must assuage
Anger's rage
As by now you understand.
If anything I have said delights you

Then that is for the best.
And so fulfil your will,
At my request

The End.

JANE ANGER
HER PROTECTION FOR WOMEN

To defend them against the scandalous reports of a late Surfeiting Lover, and all other like venerians that complaine so to bee overcloyed with womens kindnesse.

To the Gentlewomen of England, health.

Gentlewomen, though it is to be feared that your setled wits wil advisedly condemne that, which my cholloricke vaine hath rashly set downe, and so perchance, anger shal reape anger for not agreeing with diseased persons: Yet (if with indifferencie of censure, you consider of the head of the quarell) I hope you will rather shew your selves defendantes of the defenders title, then complainantes of the plaintifes wrong. I doubt judgement before trial, which were injurious to the Law, and I confesse that my rashnesse deserveth no lesse, which was a fit of my extremitie. I will not urge reasons because your wits are sharp and will soone conceive my meaning, ne will I be tedious least I proove too too troublesome, nor over darke in my writing, for feare of the name of a Ridler. But (in a worde) for my presumption I crave pardon, because it was anger that did write it: committing your protection, and my selfe, to the protection of your selves, and the judgement of the cause to the censures of your just mindes.

Yours ever at commandement,
Jane Anger

To all Women in generall and gentle Reader whatsoever: fie on the falshoode of men, whose minds goe oft a madding, & whose tongues can not so soone bee wagging, but straight they fal a railing. Was there ever any so abused, so slaundered, so railed upon, or so wickedly handeled undeservedly, as are we women? Will the Gods permit it, the Goddesses stay theyr punishing judgments, and we ourselves not pursue their undoinges for such divelish practises? O Paules steeple and Charing Crosse. A halter hold al such persons. Let the streames of the channels in London streates run so swiftly, as they may be able alone to carrie them from that sanctuarie. Let the stones be as Ice, the soales of their shooes as Glasse, the waies steep like Ætna, & every blast a Whyrl-wind puffed out of Boreas his long throat, that these may hasten their passage to the Devils haven. Shal Surfeiters raile on our kindnes, you stand stil & say nought, and shall not Anger stretch the vaines of her braines, the stringes of her fingers, and the listes of her modestie, to answere their Surfeitings? Yes truely. And herein I conjure all you to aide and assist me in defence of my willingnes, which shall make me rest at your commaundes. Fare you well.

Your friend,
Ja. A.

A Protection for Women. &c.

The desire that every man hath to shewe his true vaine in writing is unspeakable, and their mindes are so caried away with the manner, as no care at all is had of the matter: they run so into Rethorick, as often times they overrun the boundes of their own wits, and goe they knowe not whether. If they have stretched their invention so hard on a last, as it is at a stand, there remaines but one help, which is, to write of us women: If they may once encroch so far into our presence, as they may but see the lyning of our outermost garment, they straight think that Apollo honours them, in yeelding so good a supply to refresh their sore overburdened heads, through studying for matters to indite off. And therfore that the God may see how thankfully they receive his liberality, (their wits whetted, and their braines almost broken with botching his bountie) they fall straight to dispraising and slaundering our silly sex. But judge what the cause should be, of this their so great malice towards simple women. Doubtles the weakenesse of our wits, and our honest bashfulnesse, by reason wherof they suppose that there is not one amongst us who can, or dare reproove their slanders and false reproches: their slaunderous tongues are so short, and the time wherin they have lavished out their wordes freely, hath bene so long, that they know we cannot catch hold of them to pull them out, and they think we wil not write to reproove their lying lips: which conceites have already made them cockes and wolde (should they not be cravened) make themselves among themselves bee thought to be of the game. They have bene so daintely fed with our good natures, that like jades (their stomackes are grown so quesie) they surfeit of our kindnes. If we wil not suffer them to smell on our smockes, they will snatch at our peticotes: but if our honest natures cannot away with that uncivil kinde of jesting then we are coy: yet if we beare with their rudenes, and be somwhat modestly familiar with them, they will straight make matter of nothing, blazing abroad that they have surfeited with love, and then their wits must be showen in telling the maner how.

Among the innumerable number of bookes to that purpose, of late (unlooked for) the newe surfeit of an olde Lover (sent abroad to warne those which are of his own kind, from catching the like disease) came by chance to my handes: which, because as well women as men are desirous of novelties, I willinglie read over: neither did the ending thereof lesse please me then the beginning, for I was so carried away with the conceit of the Gent. as that I was quite out of the booke before I thought I had bene in the middest thereof: So pithie were his sentences, so pure his wordes, and so pleasing his stile. The chiefe matters therein contained were of two sortes: the one in the dispraise of mans follie, and the other, invective against our sex, their folly proceeding of their own flatterie joined with fancie, & our faultes are through our follie, with which is some faith.

The bounteous wordes written over the lascivious kinge Ninus his head, set down in this olde Lover his Surfeit to be these (Demaund and have:) do plainly shew the flatterie of mens false heartes: for knowing that we women, are weake vessels soone overwhelmed, and that Bountie bendeth everie thing to his becke, they take him for their instrument (too too strong) to assay the pulling downe of us so weake. If we stand fast, they strive: if we totter (though but a little) they will never leave til they have overturned us. Semeramis demaunded: and who would not if courtesie should be so freely offered? Ninus gave all to his kingdome, and that at the last: the more foole he: and of him this shal be my censure (agreeing with the verdict of the surfaiting lover, save onely that he hath misplaced and mistaken certaine wordes) in this maner.

Fooles force such flatterie, and men of dull conceite:
Such phrensie oft doth hant the wise (Nurse Wisedom once rejected)
Though love be sure and firme: yet Lust fraught with deceit,
And mens fair wordes do worke great wo, unlesse they be suspected.
Then foolish Ninus had but due, if I his judge might be,

Vilde are mens lustes, false are their lips, besmer'd with flatterie:
Himselfe and Crowne he brought to thrall which passed all the rest
His foot-stoole match he made his head, and therefore was a beast.
Then all such beastes such beastly endes, I wish the Gods to send,
And worser too if woorse may be: like his my censure end.

The slouthful king Sardanapalus with his beastlike and licentious deedes are so plainly disciphered, and his bad end well deserved, so truly set down in that Surfeit, as both our judgments agree in one.

But that Menalaus was served with such sauce it is a wonder: yet truely their Sex are so like to Buls, that it is no marvell though the Gods do metamorphoze some of them, to give warning to the rest, if they coulde think so of it, for some of them wil follow the smocke as Tom Bull will runne after a towne Cowe. But, least they should running slip and breake their pates, the Gods provident of their welfare, set a paire of tooters on their foreheades, to keepe it from the ground, for doubtles so stood the case with Menalus, hee running abroade as a Smel-smocke, got the habit of a Coockold, of whom thus shall go my verdicte:

The Gods most just doe justly punish sinne
with those same plagues which men do most forlorn,

If filthy lust in men to spring begin,
That monstrous sin he plagueth with the horne,
their wisdome great wherby they men forewarne,
to shun vild lust, lest they wil weare the horne.
Deceitfull men with guile must be repaid,
And blowes for blowes who renders not againe?
The man that is of Coockolds lot affraid,
From Lechery he ought for to refraine.
Els shall he have the plague he doth forlorne:
and ought perforce constrain'd to wear the horne.
The Greeke, Acteons badge did weare, they say,
And worthy too, he loved the smocke so wel,
That everie man may be a Bull I pray,
Which loves to follow lust (his game) so well.
For by that meanes poore women shall have peace
and want these jarres. Thus doth my censure cease.

The greatest fault that doth remaine in us women is, that we are too credulous, for could we flatter as they can dissemble, and use our wittes well, as they can their tongues ill, then never would any of them complaine of surfeiting. But if we women be so so perillous cattell as they terme us, I marvell that the Gods made not Fidelitie as well a man, as they created her a woman, and all the morall vertues of their masculine sex, as of the feminine kinde, except their Deities knewe that there was some soverainty in us women, which could not be in them men. But least some snatching fellow should catch me before I fall to the grounde, (and say they will adorne my head with a feather, affirming that I rome beyond reason, seeing it is most manifest that the man is the head of the woman, and that therfore we ought to be guided by them,) I prevent them with this answere. The Gods knowing that the mindes of mankind would be aspiring, and having throughly viewed the wonderfull vertues wherewith women are inriched, least they should provoke us to pride, and so confound us with Lucifer, they bestowed the supremacy over us to man, that of that Cockscombe he might onely boast, and therfore for Gods sake let them keepe it. But wee returne to the Surfeit.

Having made a long discourse of the Gods censure concerning love, he leaves them (& I them with him) and comes to the principall object and generall foundation of love, which he affirmeth to be grounded on women: & now beginning to search his scroule, wherein are tauntes against us, he beginneth and saieth that we allure their hearts to us: wherin he saieth more truly then he is aware off: for we woo them with our vertues, & they wed us with vanities, and men being of wit sufficient to consider of the vertues which are in us women, are ravished with the delight of those dainties, which allure & draw the sences of them to serve us, wherby they become ravenous haukes, who doe not onely seize upon us, but devour us. Our good toward them is the destruction of our selves, we being wel formed, are by them fouly deformed: of our true meaning they make mockes, rewarding our loving follies with disdainful floutes: we are the griefe of man, in that wee take all the griefe from man: we languish when they laugh, we lie sighing when they sit singing, and sit sobbing when they lie slugging and sleeping. Mulier est hominis confusio, because her kinde heart cannot so sharply reproove their franticke fits, as those madde frensies deserve. *Aut amat, aut odit, non est in tertio*: she loveth good thinges, and hateth that which is evill: shee loveth justice and hateth iniquitie: she loveth trueth and true dealing, and hateth lies and falshood: she loveth man for his vertues, & hateth him for his vices: to be short, there is no Medium between good and bad, and therefore she can be, *In nullo tertio*.

Plato his answere to a Viccar of fooles which asked the question, being, that he knew not whether to place women among those creatures which were reasonable or unreasonable, did as much beautifie his devine knowledge, as all the bookes he did write: for knowing that women are the greatest help that men have, without whose aide & assistance it is as possible for them to live, as if they wanted meat, drinke, clothing, or any other necessary: and knowing also that even then in his age, much more in those ages which shold after follow, men were grown to be so unreasonable, as he could not discide whether men or bruite beastes were more reasonable: their eies are so curious, as be not all women equall with Venus for beautie, they cannot abide the sight of them: their stomackes so queasie, as doe they tast but twise of one dish they straight surfeit, and needes must a new diet be provided for them. Wee are contrary to men, because they are contrarie to that which is good: because they are spurblind, they cannot see into our natures, and we too well (though we had but halfe an eie) into their conditions, because they are so bad: our behaviours alter daily, because mens vertues decay hourely.

If Hesiodus had with equity as well looked into the life of man, as he did presisely search out the qualities of us women, he would have said, that if a woman trust unto a man, it shal fare as well with her, as if she had a waight of a thousand pounds tied about her neck, and then cast into the bottomles seas: for by men are we confounded though they by us are sometimes crossed. Our tongues are light, because earnest in reprooving mens filthy vices, and our good counsel is termed nipping injurie, in that it accordes not with their foolish fancies. Our boldnesse rash, for giving Noddies nipping answeres, our dispositions naughtie, for not agreeing with their vilde mindes, and our furie dangerous, because it will not beare with their knavish behaviours.

If our frownes be so terrible, and our anger so deadly, men are too foolish in offering occasions of hatred, which shunned, a terrible death is prevented. There is a continuall deadly hatred betweene the wilde boare and tame hounds, I would there were the like betwixt women and men unles they amend their maners, for so strength should predominate, where now flattery and dissimulation hath the upper hand. The Lion rageth when he is hungrie, but man raileth when he is glutted. The Tyger is robbed of her young ones, when she is ranging abroad, but men rob women of their honour undeservedlye under their noses. The Viper stormeth when his taile is trodden on, & may not we fret when al our bodie is a footstoole to their vild lust: their unreasonable mindes which knowe not what reason is, make them nothing better then bruit beastes.

But let us graunt that Cletemnestra, Ariadna, Dalila, and Jesabell were spotted with crimes: shal not Nero with others innumerable, & therefore unnameable joine handes with them and lead the daunce? yet it greeves me that faithful Deianira should be falsely accused of her husband Hercules death, seeing she was utterly guiltlesse (even of thought) concerning any such crime, for had not the Centaures falshood exceeded the simplicitie of her too too credulous heart, Hercules had not died so cruelly tormented, nor the monsters treason bene so unhappely executed. But we must beare with these faultes, and with greater then these, especiallye seeing that hee which set it downe for a Maxime was driven into a mad mood through a surfeit, which made him run quite besides his booke, and mistake his case: for wher he accused Deianira falsely, he woulde have had condemned Hercules deservedly.

Marius daughter indued with so many excellent vertues, was too good either for Metellus, or any man living: for thogh peradventure she had some smal fault, yet doubtles he had detestable crimes. On the same place where Doun is on the hens head, the Combe grows on the Cocks pate. If women breede woe to men, they bring care, povertie, griefe, and continual feare to women, which if they be not woes they are worser.

Euthydemus made sixe kinde of women, and I will approove that there are so many of men: which be, poore and rich, bad and good, foule and faire. The great Patrimonies that wealthy men leave their children after their death, make them rich: but dice and other marthriftes happening into their companies, never leave them til they bee at the beggers bush, wher I can assure you they become poore. Great eaters beeing kept at a slender diet never distemper their bodies but remaine in good case: but afterwards once turned foorth to Liberties pasture, they graze so greedilie, as they become surfeiting jades, and alwaies after are good for nothing. There are men which are snout-faire, whose faces looke like a creame-pot, and yet those not the faire men I speake of, but I meane those whose conditions are free from knaverie, and I tearme those foule, that have neither civilitie nor honestie: of these sorts there are none good, none rich or faire long. But if wee doe desire to have them good, we must alwaies tie them to the manger and diet their greedy panches, other wise they wil surfeit. What, shal I say? wealth makes them lavish, wit knavish, beautie effeminate, povertie deceitfull, and deformitie uglie. Therefore of me take this counsell:

Esteeme of men as of a broken Reed,
Mistrust them still, and then you wel shall speede.

I pray you then (if this be true, as it truely cannot bee denied) have not they reason who affirme that a goose standing before a ravenous Fox, is in as good case, as the woman that trusteth to a mans fidelitie: for as the one is sure to loose his head, so the other is most certaine to be bereaved of her good name, if there be any small cause of suspition. The fellow that tooke his wife for his crosse, was an Asse, and so we will leave him: for he loved well to sweare on an ale pot, and because his wife, keeping him from his dronken vain, put his nose out of his socket, he thereby was brought into a mad moode, in which he did he could not tell what.

When provender prickes, the jade will winch, but keepe him at a slender ordinarie, and he will be milde ynough. The Dictators sonne was cranke as long as his cocke was crowing, but prooving a cravin, hee made his maister hang downe his head.

Thales was so maried to shamefull lust as hee cared not a straw for lawfull love, wherby he shewed himselfe to be indued with much vice and no vertue: for a man doth that often times standing, of which he repenteth sitting. The Romain coulde not (as now men cannot) abide to heare women praised, and themselves dispraised, and therfore it is best for men to follow Alfonso his rule: let them be deafe and mary wives, that are blind, so shal they not grieve to heare their wives commended nor their monstrous misdoing shall offend their wives eiesight.

Tibullus setting down a rule for women to follow, might

have proportioned this platform for men to rest in. And might have said, Every honest man ought to shun that which detracteth both health and safety from his owne person, and strive to bridle his slanderous tongue. Then must he be modest, & shew his modestie by his vertuous and civil behaviours: and not display his beastlines through his wicked and filthy wordes. For lying lips and deceitful tongues are abhominable before God. It is an easie matter to intreate a Cat to catch a Mouse, and more easie to perswade a desperate man to kil him selfe. What Nature hath made, Art cannot marre, (and as this surfeiting lover saith) that which is bred in the bone, will not be brought out of the flesh. If we cloath our selves in sackcloth, and trusse up our haire in dishclouts, Venerians wil nevertheles pursue their pastime. If we hide our breastes, it must be with leather, for no cloath can keep their long nailes out of our bosomes.

We have rowling eies, and they railing tongues: our eies cause them to look lasciviously, & why? because they are geven to lecherie. It is an easie matter to finde a staffe to beate a Dog, and a burnt finger giveth sound counsel. If men would as well imbrace counsel as they can give it, Socrates rule wold be better follewed. But let Socrates, heaven and earth say what they wil, Mans face is worth a glasse of dissembling water: and therfore to conclude with a proverbe, Write ever, and yet never write ynough of mans falshoode, I meane those that use it. I would that ancient writers would as well have busied their heades about discipheringe the deceites of their owne Sex, as they have about setting downe our follies: and I wold some would call in question that nowe, which hath ever bene questionlesse: but sithence all their wittes have bene bent to write of the contrarie, I leave them to a contrary vaine, and the surfaiting Lover, who returnes to his discourse of love.

Nowe while this greedye grazer is about his intreatie of love, which nothing belongeth to our matter: let us secretlye our selves with our selves, consider howe and in what, they that are our worst enemies, are both inferiour unto us, & most beholden unto our kindenes.

The creation of man and woman at the first, hee being formed In principio of drosse and filthy clay, did so remaine until God saw that in him his workmanship was good, and therfore by the transformation of the dust which was loathsome unto flesh, it became purified. Then lacking a help for him, GOD making woman of mans fleshe, that she might bee purer then he, doth evidently showe, how far we women are more excellent then men. Our bodies are fruitefull, wherby the world encreaseth, and our care wonderful, by which man is preserved. From woman sprang mans salvation. A woman was the first that beleeved, & a woman likewise the first that repented of sin. In women is onely true Fidelity: (except in her) there is constancie, and without her no Huswifery. In the time of their sicknes we cannot be wanted, & when they are in health we for them are most necessary. They are comforted by our means: they nourished by the meats we dresse: their bodies freed from diseases by our cleanlines, which otherwise would surfeit unreasonably through their own noisomnes. Without our care they lie in their beds as dogs in litter, & goe like lowsie Mackarell swimming in the heat of sommer. They love to go hansomly in their apparel, and rejoice in the pride thereof, yet who is the cause of it, but our carefulnes, to see that every thing about them be curious. Our virginitie makes us vertuous, our conditions curteous, & our chastitie maketh our truenesse of love manifest. They confesse we are necessarie, but they would have us likewise evil. That they cannot want us I grant: yet evill I denie: except onely in the respect of man, who, hating all good things, is onely desirous of that which is ill, through whose desire, in estimation of conceit we are made ill. But least some shuld snarle on me, barking out this reason: that none is good but God, and therfore women are ill. I must yeeld that in that respect we are il, & affirm that men are no better, seeing we are so necessarie unto them. It is most certain, that if we be il, they are worse: for *Malum malo additum efficit malum peius*: & they that use il worse then it shold be, are worse then the il. And therefore if they wil correct Magnificat, they must first learn the signification therof. That we are liberal, they wil not deny sithence that many of them have (*ex confessio*) received more kindnes in one day at our hands, then they can repay in a whole yeare: & some have so glutted themselves with our liberality as they cry No more. But if they shal avow that women are fooles, we may safely give them the lie: for my selfe have heard some of them confesse that we have more wisdome then need is, & therfore no fooles: & they lesse then they shold have, & therfore fooles. It hath bene affirmed by some of their sex, that to shun a shower of rain, & to know the way to our husbands bed is wisedome sufficient for us women: but in this yeare of 88, men are grown so fantastical, that unles we can make them fooles, we are accounted unwise. And now (seeing I speake to none but to you which are of mine owne Sex,) give me leave like a scoller to proove our wisdome more excellent then theirs, though I never knew what sophistry ment. Ther is no wisdome but it comes by grace, this is a principle, & *Contra principium non est disputandum*: but grace was first given to a woman, because to our lady: which premises conclude that women are wise. Now *Primum est optimum*, & therefore women are wiser then men. That we are more witty which comes by nature, it cannot better be prooved, then that by our answers, men are often droven to Non plus, & if their talk be of worldly affaires, with our resolutions they must either rest satisfied, or proove themselves fooles in the end.

It was my chance to hear a prety story of two wise men who (being cosen germane to the town of Gotam) prooved themselves as very asses, as they wer fooles: & it was this. The stelth of a ring out of a wise mans chamber, afflicted the loosers mind, with so grievous passions, as he could take no rest, til he went to aske a friends counsel, how he might recover his losse. Into whose presence being once entered, his clothes unbuttoned, made passage for his friends eiesight unto his bosome: who seeing him in such a taking, judging by his looks that some qualme had risen on his stomack, the extremity wherof might make his head to ake, offered him a kertcher. This distressed man halfe besides himselfe, howled bitterly that he did mistake his case, & falling into a raving vain, began to curse the day of his birth, & the Destinies for suffering him to live. His fellow wise-man, mistaking this fit, fearing that some devil had possessed him, began to betake him to his heeles: but being stopped from running by his companion, did likewise ban the cause of this suddain change, & the motion that mooved the other to enter his presence: yet seing how daungerously he was disturbed, &

knowing that by no meanes he could shun his company, calling his wittes together (which made him forget his passion) he demanded the cause of the others griefe: who taking a stoole & a cushion sate downe and declared that he was undone through the losse of a ring which was stolen out of his window: further saying, Sir, is it not best for mee to goe to a Wise-woman to knowe of her what is become of my ring? The other answering affirmatively, asked this: if he know anye? betweene whom, many wise women reckoned, they both went together for company, wher we wil leave them.

Now I pray you tell me your fancie, were not these men very wise, but especially did they not cunningly display their wisedome by this practise? Sithence that they hope to finde that through the wisedome of a woman, which was lost by the folly of a man. Wel, seeing according to the old proverb: The wit of a woman is a great matter: let men learne to be wiser or account them selves fooles: for they know by practize that we are none.

Now sithence that this overcloied and surfeiting lover leaveth his love, and comes with a fresh assault against us women let us arm our selves with patience & see the end of his tongue which explaineth his surfeit. But it was so lately printed, as that I shold do the Printer injurie should I recite but one of them, and therfore referring you to Boke his surfeit in love, I come to my matter. If to injoy a woman be to catch the Devill by the foote, to obtaine the favour of a man is to holde fast his damme by the middle: whereby the one may easily breake away, and the other cannot go without he carries the man with him.

The properties of the Snake and of the Eele are, the one to sting, and the other not to be held: but mens tongues sting against nature, and therefore they are unnaturall. Let us bear with them as much as may be, and yeeld to their willes more then is convenient: yet if we cast our reckoning at the end of the yeare, wee shall finde that our losses exceede their gaines, which are innumerable. The propertie of the Camelion is to change himselfe: But man alwaies remaineth at one stay, and is never out of the predicamentes of Dishonestie and unconstancie. The stinging of the Scorpion is cured by the Scorpion, wherby it seemes that there is some good nature in them. But men never leave stinging till they see the death of honestie. The danger of prickes is shunned, by gathering roses glove fisted: and the stinging of Bees prevented through a close hood. But naked Dishonestie and bare inconstancie are alwaies plagued through their owne follie.

If mens folly be so unreasonable as it will strive against Nature, it is no matter though she rewardes them with crosses contrary to their expectations. For if Tom foole will presume to ride on Alexanders horse, he is not to be pittied thogh he get a foule knocke for his labour. But it seemes the Gentleman hath had great experience of Italian Curtizans, wherby his wisedome is shewed. For *Experientia præstantior arte*: and hee that hath Experience to proove his case, is in better case then they that have al unexperienced book cases to defend their titles.

The smooth speeches of men are nothing unlike the vanishing cloudes of the Aire, which glide by degrees from place to place, till they have filled themselves with raine, when breaking, they spit foorth terrible showers: so men gloze, till they have their answeres, which are the end of their travell, & then they bid Modestie adue, and entertaining Rage, fal a railing on us which never hurt them. The rancknesse of grasse causeth suspition of the serpents lurking, but his lying in the plaine path at the time when Woodcockes shoote, maketh the pacient passionate through his sting, because no such ill was suspected. When men protest secrecie most solemnly, beleeve them lest, for then surely there is a tricke of knavery to be discarded, for in a Friers habite an olde Fornicator is alwaies clothed.

It is a wonder to see how men can flatter themselves with their own conceites: for let us looke, they wil straight affirm that we love, and if then Lust pricketh them, they will sweare that Love stingeth us: which imagination onely is sufficient to make them assay the scaling of halfe a dozen of us in one night, when they will not stick to sweare that if they should be denied of their requestes, death must needes follow. Is it any marvell though they surfeit, when they are so greedy, but is it not pittie that any of them should perish, which will be so soon killed with unkindnes? Yes truly. Well, the onset given, if we retire for a vantage, they will straight affirme that they have got the victorie. Nay, some of them are so carried away with conceite, that shameles they wil blaze abroad among their companions, that they have obteined the love of a woman, unto whom they never spake above once, if that: Are not these forward fellowes, you must beare with them, because they dwell far from lying neighboures. They will say *Mentiri non est nostrum*, and yet you shall see true tales come from them, as wilde geese flie under London bridge. Their fawning is but flattery: their faith falshoode: their faire wordes allurements to destruction: and their large promises tokens of death, or of evils worse then death. Their singing is a bayte to catch us, and their playinges, plagues to torment us: & therfore take heede of them, and take this as an Axiom in Logick and a Maxime in the Law, *Nulla fides hominibus*. Ther are three accidents to men, which of al are most unseperable. Lust, Deceit, and malice. Their glozing tongues, the preface to the execution of their vilde mindes, and their pennes the bloody executioners of their barbarous maners. A little gaule maketh a great deale of sweet, sower: and a slaunderous tongue poysoneth all the good partes in man.

Was not the follie of Vulcan worthy of Venus floutes, when she tooke him with the maner, wooing Briceris? And was it not the flatterye of Paris which intysed Hellen to falshood? Yes trulie: and the late Surfeiter his remembrance in calling his pen from raging against reason: sheweth that he is not quite without flatterie, for hee putteth the fault in his pen, when it was his passion that deserved reproofe. The love of Hipsicrates and Panthea, the zeale of Artemisia and Portia, the affection of Sulpitia and Aria, the true fancie of Hipparchia and Pisca, the loving passions of Macrina & of the wife of Pandoerus (al manifested in his Surfeit) shal condemne the undiscreetnes of mens minds: whose hearts delight in nought, save that only which is contrary to good. Is it not a foolish thing to bee sorry for things unrecoverable? Why then shold Sigismundus answer be so descanted upon, seeing her husband was dead, & she therby free for any man. Of the aboundance of the hart, the mouth speaketh, which is verified by the railing kind of mans writing. Of al kind of voluptuousnes, they affirm Lechery to be the cheefest, & yet some of them are not ashamed to confesse publiquely, that they have surfeited therwith. It defileth the body, & makes it stink, & men use it: I marvel how we women can abide them but that they delude us, as (they say) we deceive them with perfumes.

Voluptuousnes is a strong beast, and hath many instruments to draw to Lust: but men are so forward of themselves thereto, as they neede none to haile them. His court is already so full with them, that he hath more neede to make stronger gates to keepe them out, then to set them open that they may come in, except he wil be pulled out by the eares out of his kingdome. I woulde the abstinence of King Cyrus, Zenocrates, Caius Gracchus, Pompeius and of Francis Sforce Duke of Millaine, (recited in Boke his Surfeit in love) might be presidents for men to followe, and I warrant you then we should have no surfeiting. I pray God that they may mend: but in the meane time, let them be sure that rashnes breedes repentance, and treacherous hearts, tragical endes: false Flattery is the messenger of foule Folly, and a slaunderous tongue, the instrument of a dissembling heart.

I have set down unto you (which are of mine owne Sex) the subtil dealings of untrue meaning men: not that you should contemne al men, but to the end that you may take heed of the false hearts of al, & stil reproove the flattery which remaines in all: for as it is reason that the Hennes should be served first, which both lay the egs, & hatch the chickins: so it were unreasonable that the cockes which tread them, should be kept clean without meat. As men are valiant, so are they vertuous: and those that are borne honorably, cannot beare horrible dissembling heartes. But as there are some which cannot love hartely, so there are many who lust uncessantly, & as many of them wil deserve wel, so most care not how il they spæd so they may get our company. Wherin they resemble Envie, who will be contented to loose one of his eies that another might have both his pulled out. And therefore thinke well of as many as you may, love them that you have cause, heare every thing that they say, (& affoord them noddes which make themselves noddies) but beleeve very little therof or nothing at all, and hate all those, who shall speake any thing in the dispraise or to the dishonor of our sex.

Let the luxurious life of Heliogabalus, the intemperate desires of Commodus and Proculus, the damnable lust of Chilpericus and Xerxees, Boleslaus violent ravishings, and the unnaturall carnall appetite of Sigismundus Malotesta, be examples sufficiently probable to perswade you, that the hearts of men are most desirous to excell in vice. There were many good lawes established by the Romanes & other good kinges yet they coulde not restraine men from lecherie: and there are terrible lawes alotted in England to the offenders therein, all which will not serve to restrain man.

The Surfeiters phisike is good could he and his companions follow it: but when the fox preacheth, let the geese take heede, it is before an execution. *Fallere fallentem non est fraus*, and to kill that beast, whose propertie is onely to slay, is no sin: if you wil please men, you must follow their rule, which is to flatter: for Fidelitie and they are bitter enemies. Things far fetched are excellent, and that experience is best which cost most: Crownes are costly, and that which cost many crownes is wel worth God thank you, or els I know who hath spent his labour and cost, foolishly. Then if any man geveth such deare counsell gratfuly, are not they fooles which will refuse his liberalitie. I know you long to heare what that counsel should be, which was bought at so hie a price: Wherefore if you listen, the Surfeiter his pen with my hande shall foorthwith shew you.

At the end of mens faire promises there is a Laberinth, & therefore ever hereafter stoppe your eares when they protest friendship, lest they come to an end before you are aware wherby you fal without redemption. The path which leadeth therunto, is Mans wit, and the miles ends are marked with these trees, Follie, Vice, Mischiefe, Lust, Deceite, & Pride. These to deceive you shall bee clothed in the raimentes of Fancie, Vertue, Modestie, Love, Truemeaning, and Handsomnes. Folly wil bid you welcome on your way, & tel you his fancie, concerning the profite which may come to you by this jorney, and direct you to Vice who is more craftie. He with a company of protestations will praise the vertues of women, shewing how many waies men are beholden unto us: but our backes once turned, he fals a railing. Then Mischiefe he pries into every corner of us, seeing if he can espy a cranny, that getting in his finger into it, he may make it wide enough for his tong to wag in. Now being come to Lust: he will fall a railing on lascivious lookes, & wil ban Lecherie, & with the Collier will say, the devill take him though he never means it. Deceit will geve you faire words, & pick your pockets: nay he will pluck out your hearts, if you be not wary. But when you heare one cry out against lawnes, drawn-workes, Periwigs, against the attire of Curtizans, & generally of the pride of al women: then know him for a Wolfe clothed in sheepes raiment, and be sure you are fast by the lake of destruction. Therfore take heed of it, which you shall doe, if you shun mens flattery, the forerunner of our undoing. If a jade be galled, wil he not winch? and can you finde fault with a horse that springeth when he is spurred? The one will stand quietly when his backe is healed, and the other go wel when his smart ceaseth. You must beare with the olde Lover his surfeit, because hee was diseased when he did write it, and peradventure hereafter, when he shal be well amended, he wil repent himselfe of his slanderous speaches against our sex, and curse the dead man which was the cause of it, and make a publique recantation: For the faltering in his speach at the latter end of his book affirmeth, that already he half repenteth of his bargaine, & why? because his melodie is past: but beleeve him not, thogh he shold out swear you, for althogh a jade may be still in a stable when his gall backe is healed, yet hee will showe himselfe in his kind when he is travelling: and mans flattery bites secretly, from which I pray God keepe you and me too.

Amen.

Finis.

A soveraigne Salve, to cure the late Surfeiting Lover.
If once the heat, did fore thee beat,
    of foolish love so blind:
Somtime to sweat, somtime to freat
    as one bestraught of minde:
If wits weare take, in such a brake,
    that reason was exilde:
And woe did wake, but could not slake
    thus love had thee beguilde:

If any wight, unto thy sight,
  all other did excell:
whose beautie bright, constrained right
  thy heart with her to dwell:
If thus thy foe, opprest thee so,
  that backe thou could not start:
But still with woe, did surfeit thoe,
  yet thankles was thy smart:
If nought but paine, in love remaine,
  at length this counsell win,
That thou refrain, this dangerous pain,
  and come no more therein.
And sith the blast, is overpast,
  it better were certaine:
From flesh to fast, whilst life doth last,
  then surfeit so againe.
Vivendo disce.
Jo. A.

Eiusdem ad Lectorem, de Authore.
Though, sharpe the seede, by Anger sowen,
  we all (almost) confesse:
And hard his hap we aye account,
  who Anger doth possesse:

Yet haplesse shalt thou (Reader) reape,
 such fruit from ANGERS soile,
As may thee please, and ANGER ease
 from long and wearie toile
Whose paines were tooke for thy behoofe,
 to till that cloddye ground,
Where scarce no place, free from disgrace,
 of female Sex, was found.
If ought offend, which she doth send,
 impute it to her moode.
For ANGERS rage must that asswage,
 as wel is understoode
If to delight, ought come in sight,
 then deeme it for the best.
So you your wil, may well fulfill,
 and she have her request.

Finis.

Jo. A.

NOTES

NOTES

1. Investors in People is a framework for developing and managing the employees of a company. In 1990, the Department of Employment was charged with developing a national standard of good practice for training and development. Investors in People was officially launched at that year's CBI Conference in Glasgow by then Secretary of State for Employment, the Rt Hon Michael Howard QC MP.

2. Jane Anger's work responds to a misogynistic pamphlet - probably the anonymous (and now lost) *Book his Surfeit in Love*. The book was printed by Thomas Orwin and may well have been authored by Orwin himself. Jane Anger refers to the authorial voice in Orwin's pamphlet as 'the surfeiting lover', rendered in this modern English edition as 'the over-indulging lover'.

3. Boreas was the Greek god of the cold north wind and the bringer of winter. He was frequently depicted as a winged old man with shaggy hair and beard, wearing a billowing cloak and holding a conch shell.

4. Apollo is one of the most important and complex of the Olympian deities in classical Greek and Roman mythology. He has been represented as a god of archery, music and dance, truth and prophecy, healing and diseases, the sun and light, poetry, and more.

5. According to Greek historians, King Ninus was accepted as the eponymous founder of Nineveh, ancient capital of Assyria. He does not seem to represent any one historical figure and is most likely a conflation of several real and/or fictional figures of antiquity.

6. King Ninus waged war against Oxyartes, King of Bactriana, conquering all but the capital, Bactra. During the siege of Bactra, he met Semiramis who was the wife of one of his officers, Onnes. Ninus lured Semiramis away from her husband and married her.

7. According to the Greek writer Ctesias, Sardanapalus was the last king of Assyria. He is portrayed as a decadent figure who spent his whole life in self-indulgence. He dressed in women's clothes and wore makeup. He had many concubines, female and male. He wrote his

own epitaph, declaring that physical gratification is the only purpose of life.

8. The Trojan War was waged against the city of Troy after Paris of Troy took Helen from her husband Menelaus, King of Sparta. The war is one of the most important events in Greek mythology and has been narrated through many works of Greek literature, most notably Homer's *Iliad*.

9. The horns on a bull's head resemble the headdress worn by a court jester or fool. This would have been an instantly recognisable image in Jane Anger's time, denoting someone who had been cuckolded, or fooled in love, by an unfaithful wife.

10. According to the Roman poet Ovid, Artemis turned Actaeon into a stag because he accidentally caught sight of her bathing on Mount Cithaeron. His horns, then, were his 'badge' making him resemble a cuckold or someone who had been deceived by a lover.

11. Hera was the wife of Zeus and queen of the ancient Greek gods. She represented the ideal woman and was the goddess of marriage and the family. She was notable as one of the very few deities that remained faithful to her partner and she therefore came to symbolise monogamy and fidelity.

12. Hesiod was one of the earliest Greek poets thought to be active between 750 and 650 BC and a contemporary of Homer. Two of his epic poems survive in their entirety: the *Theogony*, relating the myths of the gods, and the *Works and Days*, describing peasant life. In *Works and Days*, Hesiod recounts two myths illustrating the necessity for honest, hard work in man's wretched life. One continues the story of Pandora, who out of curiosity opens a jar, loosing multifarious evils on humanity; the other traces man's decline since the Golden Age.

13. In Greek mythology, Clytemnestra was the wife of Agamemnon, King of Mycenae, and the sister of Helen of Troy. In Aeschylus' *Oresteia*, she murders Agamemnon (her second husband according to

Euripides) and the Trojan princess Cassandra, whom Agamemnon had taken as a war prize following the sack of Troy.

14. Ariadne was the daughter of Pasiphae and the Cretan king Minos. She fell in love with the Athenian hero Theseus and helped him escape from the Labyrinth after he had killed the Minotaur, a beast half-bull and half-man that Minos kept in the Labyrinth. In one version of the legend, she is abandoned by Theseus and hangs herself in despair.

15. Delilah appears in the Bible (Judges 16). She is loved by Samson, a Nazirite who possesses great strength and serves as the final Judge of Israel. Delilah is bribed by the lords of the Philistines to discover the source of his strength. She goads Samson into telling her that his strength is derived from his hair. As he sleeps, Delilah orders a servant to cut Samson's hair, thereby enabling her to turn him over to the Philistines.

16. Jezebel was the daughter of Ithobaal I of Sidon and the wife of Ahab, King of Israel. According to the Bible (Kings 16:31), Jezebel incited her husband King Ahab to abandon the worship of Yahweh and promote the national worship of the deities Baal and Asherah. For her transgressions against God and the people of Israel, Jezebel met a gruesome death, thrown out of a window by members of her own court, her corpse eaten by stray dogs. In some interpretations of the Biblical narrative, her use of makeup led to the association of the 'painted women' and prostitution.

17. Nero Claudius Caesar Augustus Germanicus (15 December 37 AD - 9 June 68 AD) was the last Roman emperor of the Julio-Claudian dynasty. Most Roman sources are negative about his personality and reign. Tacitus claims that the Roman people thought him compulsive and corrupt. Suetonius suggests many Romans believed that the Great Fire of Rome was instigated by Nero to clear the way for his planned palatial complex, the *Domus Aurea*. According to Tacitus, he was said to have seized Christians as scapegoats for the fire and burned them alive, motivated by pure cruelty.

NOTES

18. Deianira was a Calydonian princess in Greek mythology whose name translated as 'man-destroyer' or 'destroyer of her husband'. She was the wife of Heracles and, in late Classical accounts, his unwitting murderer. Fearing that Heracles had taken a new lover, Deianeira gives him a shirt stained with the blood of the centaur Nessus. She had been tricked by the dying Nessus into believing it would serve as a potion to ensure her husband's faithfulness. In fact, it contained the venom of the Lernaean Hydra. When Heracles puts on the shirt, the Hydra's venom begins to cook him alive, and to escape the unbearable pain he builds a funeral pyre and throws himself on it.

19. Walter Map's *Dissuasio Valerii ad Rufinum philosophum ne uxorem ducat (The Advice of Valerius to Rufinus not to Marry)* 1180-1183, details the disadvantages of marriage and illustrates the unhappiness that lies in store, the author claims, for any man who marries. 'In choosing a wife four things compel men to love: beauty, family, wealth, and moral behaviour.' According to Map, Marius's daughter was excellent in all four.

20. Quintus Caecilius Metellus Numidicus (died c. 91 BC) was the leader of the conservative faction of the Roman Senate and a bitter enemy of Gaius Marius. He was the chief commander in the Jugurthine War in Numidia until Marius displaced him. Metellus later became censor, the magistrate responsible for the census and for public morality. In 102 BC he attempted to remove the reformers Lucius Appuleius Saturninus and Gaius Servilius Glaucia from the Senate, and failed. He went into exile rather than support legislation put forward by Saturninus.

21. *Euthydemus*, written c. 384 BC, is a dialogue in which Plato satirises the intellectuals and teachers known as sophists. Socrates describes to his friend Crito a visit he and various youths paid to two prominent sophists, Euthydemus and Dionysodorus. Throughout the dialogue, they attempt to confound Socrates with deceptive and meaningless arguments, calculated to demonstrate their self-declared philosophical superiority.

NOTES

22. By 'the dictator' Anger may mean the male sex drive. Man, ('the dictator's son' in that he is governed by his sex drive) is in pain because he is sexually aroused but has no outlet. Anger suggests that if he can deal with his sexual craving in some way, he will be able to lose his painful erection. The imagery of erection and loss of erection is unmistakable.

23. Thales of Miletus was a pre-Socratic philosopher, mathematician and astronomer from Miletus in Ionia, Asia Minor. Aristotle regarded him as the first philosopher in the Greek tradition. Accounts vary as to whether or not Thales ever married. Some say he married and had a son. Others say that he never married, but treated one of his nephews as if he were his son. Anger's inference seems to be that Thales' sexual relationships must have taken place outside of marriage and are therefore morally suspect.

24. In 1455, the writer Antonio Beccadelli, aka Panormita, compiled a 'biography' of his patron Alfonso of Aaragon, who ruled Naples from 1442 until his death in 1458. This work, *De dictis et facts Alphonsi regis Aragonum (On the Words and Deeds of Alfonso King of Aragon)* is a loosely structured collection of anecdotes about the King's life and character, and contains nearly thirty of his jokes. Jane Anger is referring to one of the jokes, worded in the original as follows: *King Alfonso said a marriage could only be tranquil; and peaceful if the wife were blind and the husband deaf.*

25. Albius Tibullus (c.55 BC - 19 BC) was a Latin poet and writer of elegies. Only his first and second books of poetry are extant. Little is known about his life.

26. By the term 'Socrates' rule', Anger may mean the Socratic idea that a law may be just but it can be unjustly used.

27. In the line 'our chastity makes our truthfulness in matters of love evident', Anger refers to the now questionable idea that female virginity is physically verifiable by examination of the hymen.

28. The Magnificat (latin: '[My soul] magnifies [the Lord]') is one of the eight most ancient Christian hymns and perhaps the earliest hymn associated with the Virgin Mary:

My soul proclaims the greatness of the Lord,
my spirit rejoices in God my Saviour,
for he has looked with favour on his humble servant.
From this day all generations will call me blessed,
the Almighty has done great things for me,
and holy is his Name.
He has mercy on those who fear Him
in every generation.
He has shown the strength of his arm,
he has scattered the proud in their conceit.
He has cast down the mighty from their thrones,
and has lifted up the humble.
He has filled the hungry with good things,
and the rich he has sent away empty.
He has come to the help of his servant Israel
for he has remembered his promise of mercy,
the promise he made to our fathers,
to Abraham and his children for ever.
Glory to the Father, and to the Son, and to the Holy Spirit,
as it was in the beginning, is now, and will be for ever.
Amen.

29. The figure of Tom Fool first appears in the early 1300s in the Latinate form *Thomas Fatuus*. 'Tom' serves as a generic term for any ordinary person as in the phrase, 'Tom, Dick or Harry'. 'Fatuus' means stupid or foolish in Latin and is the root of words like 'fatuous' and 'infatuate'. By 1356, *Thomas Fatuus* had become anglicised as Tom Fool.

30. Bucephalus (meaning 'oxhead') was the horse of Alexander the Great. A massive creature with a massive head, Bucephalus is described as having a black coat with a large white star on his brow. Alexander won the horse at the age of twelve or thirteen by

successfully taming it where everyone else had failed. According to
Plutarch, he spoke soothingly to it and turned it towards the sun so
that it could no longer see its own shadow, which had been the cause
of its skittishness.

31. Anger is referring to a 1593 pamphlet *Tell-Trothes New-years Gift* with
the subtitle *Beeing Robin Good-Fellowes Newes out of those Countries where
Inhabites neither Charity nor Honesty*. The passage quoted by Anger is a
retelling of the love triangle between the Roman gods Vulcan, Venus
and Mars: *Vulcan's jealousy prevailed him nothing, and his catching of Mars
and Venus in a net as little, except confirmation of his great grief, and an
assured knowledge of his horned head, proving a continual badge of his infamy.
The like followed many others' suspicion, and the like will ensure of such folly.
Vulcan knew that Mars was a copartner with him in Venus bosom. And he
himself could not but blush when he had wooed his own spouse (the goddess of
love) in stead of Briceris, his beloved paramour.*

32. Paris is the son of King Priam and Queen Hecuba of Troy. His
elopement with Helen, Queen of Sparta, was one of the immediate
causes of the Trojan War. Helen was married to King Menelaus of
Sparta and, according to some versions of the legend, was stolen
from Menelaus' house. In alternative accounts, Helen fell in love
with Paris and left willingly. This is presumably what Anger means by
Paris' flattery.

33. Hypsicratea was the sixth and the most famous wife of Mithridates
VI, King of Pontus. She loved her husband so much that she
disguised herself as a man and rode into battle, suppressing
rebellions and fighting against the Roman Republic.

34. Panthea was the wife of Abradatas, King of Susa, described by
Xenophon in his biography of Cyrus the Great, the *Cyropaedia*.
Panthea was taken by Cyrus while Abradatas was away on a mission.
Panthea was treated so honourably by Cyrus, that Abradatas was
convinced to join forces with him. When Abradatas died in battle,
Panthea was inconsolable and committed suicide.

NOTES

35. Artemis believed that she had been chosen by the Fates to be a midwife, particularly since she had assisted her mother in the delivery of her twin brother, Apollo. All of her companions remained virgins, and Artemis closely guarded her own chastity.

36. Porcia Catonis (c. 70 BC - June 43 BC or October 42 BC) was the second wife of Marcus Junius Brutus, the most famous of Julius Caesar's assassins. To prove to her husband that she was trustworthy, she used a barber's knife to make a self-inflicted wound on her thigh. She intended to demonstrate that she could endure the pain in silence, saying to her husband: *I found that my body also can keep silence... Therefore fear not, but tell me all you are concealing from me, for neither fire, nor lashes, nor goads will force me to divulge a word.* Porcia committed suicide, reputedly by swallowing hot coals, though it is unclear whether she killed herself on hearing of Brutus' death or because she couldn't bear her long separation from him.

37. Sulpicia (fl. 113 BC) was one of 100 Roman matrons who were candidates to win the honour of dedicating a statue of Venus Verticordia. Venus Verticordia, or the changer of hearts, was believed to turn the minds of women from vice to virtue. Sulpicia was judged the most chaste of all 100 Roman matrons and selected to dedicate the statue.

38. In Greek mythology, Areia was the nymph-daughter of Cleochus of Crete and the wife of the god Apollo. When she gave birth to her son, she hid him in a bed of smilax, or briars; Cleochus found the child there and reputedly named him Miletus after the plant.

39. Hipparchia (fl. c. 325 BC) was born in Maroneia, but her family moved to Athens. There she met Crates of Thebes, the most famous Cynic philosopher in Greece at that time. She fell in love with him, and, despite the disapproval of her parents, she married him. She went on to live a life of Cynic poverty on the streets of Athens, considered scandalous for respectable women of the time. The story of her love for Crates, and her rejection of conventional values, became a popular theme for later writers.

NOTES

40. Anger is quoting from *The French Academie* (1586) by the influential French writer of the time Pierre de la Primaudaye (1546-1619): *Pisca seeing her husband pine away daily through a great and strange disease, which he had concealed from her for a long time, having at length knowledge thereof, and perceiving it to be incurable, she was moved with pity for the ill which he suffered, whom she loved better than herself: and thereupon counselled him with great courage to assuage his grief by death, and the better to stir him up thereunto, she offered to keep him company. Whereupon her husband agreeing, they embraced each other and cast themselves headlong into the sea from the top of a rock.*

41. Saint Macrina the Younger (c. 330 - 19 July 379) was a nun in the Early Christian Church and is a prominent saint in the Roman Catholic, Eastern Catholic, and Eastern Orthodox churches. Her younger brother, Saint Gregory of Nyssa, wrote about her life focusing heavily on her virginity and asceticism.

42. This is Jane Anger's second quote from *The French Academie* by Pierre de la Primaudaye (see note 40): *The King of Persia taking prisoner the wife of Pandoerus, whom he had vanquished and slain, would have married her. But she killed herself after she had uttered these words: God forbid, that to be a queen, I should ever wed him that hath been the murderer of my dear husband Pandoerus.*

43. Barbara of Cilli (1392 - 11 July 1451) was the Holy Roman Empress and Queen of Hungary and Bohemia by marriage to Holy Roman Emperor Sigismund. She was actively involved in politics and the economy of her times, independently administering large feudal fiefdoms and systems of taxation. She served as the regent of the Hungarian kingdom in the absence of her husband four times: in 1412, 1414, 1416, and 1418. She was crowned Queen of Hungary in 1408, Queen of Germany in 1414, Holy Roman Empress in 1433 and Queen of Bohemia in 1437, shortly before her husband's death. In 1409, She gave birth to a daughter, Elisabeth, Sigismund's only surviving issue and heiress. The day before the death of her gravely ill husband, her son-in-law Albert II of the Habsburg dynasty and his chancellor Kaspar Schlick accused her of plotting against

NOTES

Sigismund. She was swiftly transported to prison in Bratislava Castle and later forced to relinquish most of her possessions, including her dowry. Barbara eventually found shelter in the Polish royal court, where she lived in exile from 1438 to 1441. She spent the rest of her life as Dowager Queen in Bohemia. She seems to have retreated from political life, although the Habsburg court saw her as dangerous and tried to accuse her of heresy, alchemy, and immoral and agnostic behaviour.

44. King Cyrus II of Persia, commonly known as Cyrus the Great, was the founder of the Achaemenid Empire, the first Persian Empire. Under his rule, the empire embraced all the previous civilised states of the ancient Near East, expanded vastly and eventually conquered most of Western Asia and much of Central Asia. From the Mediterranean Sea and Hellespont in the west to the Indus River in the east, Cyrus the Great created the largest empire the world had yet seen. According to Greek Philosopher Xenophon (c. 431BC - 354 BC), the main challenge faced by the Achaemenid empire was the loss of Persian discipline: 'Men are much more effeminate now than they were in Cyrus' day. For at that time they still adhered to the old discipline and the old abstinence that they received from the Persians... now, on the contrary, they are allowing the rigour of the Persians to die out.'

45. Xenocrates (c. 396 BC - 314 BC) of Chalcedon was a Greek philosopher, mathematician, and leader of the Platonic Academy from c. 338 to 314 BC. According to Xenocrates, the Athenian hero Triptolemus was the originator of laws requiring abstinence from the slaughter and consumption of animals.

46. Gaius Sempronius Gracchus (154 - 121 BC) was a Roman politician in the 2nd Century BC and brother of the reformer Tiberius Sempronius Gracchus. His election to the office of tribune in the years 123 BC and 122 BC and his policies of reform prompted a constitutional crisis. He died in 121 BC during civil unrest attributed to drunkenness.

NOTES

47. Gnaeus Pompey Magnus (29 September 106 BC - 28 September 48 BC), known simply as Pompey, was a military and political leader of the late Roman Republic. His immense success as a general while still very young enabled him to advance directly to his first consulship without meeting the normal requirements for the office. He attained great fame in Rome for abstaining from plunder.

48. Francesco II Sforza (4 February 1495 - 24 October 1535) was Duke of Milan from 1521 until his death. He was the last member of the Sforza family to rule the Italian city. On 4 May 1534, he married the 12-year-old niece of Charles V, Christina of Denmark, the daughter of Christian II of Denmark and Isabella of Burgundy. The union remained childless.

49. Elagabalus, also known as Heliogabalus (c. 204 - 222) was emperor of Rome from 218 to 222. Later historians suggest Elagabalus showed a disregard for Roman religious traditions and sexual taboos. He was supposedly married as many as five times, lavishing favours on male courtiers, popularly thought to have been his lovers, and was reported to have prostituted himself in the imperial palace.

50. Commodus (31 August 161 - 31 December 192), was Roman emperor with his father Marcus Aurelius from 177 to his father's death in 180, and solely until 192. He thought of himself as the reincarnation of Hercules, frequently emulating the legendary hero's feats by appearing in the arena to fight a variety of wild animals. Romans found Commodus' gladiatorial combats scandalous. It was rumoured that he was not actually the son of Marcus Aurelius but of a gladiator, a lover his mother, Faustina, had taken at the coastal resort of Caieta.

51. Titus Ilius Proculus (died c. 281) was a Roman usurper, attempting to assume the power of the legitimate Emperor. Gibbon cites a letter written by Proculus in which he boast about his sexual exploits: *From Proculus to his kinsman Maecianus, greeting. I have taken one hundred maidens from Sarmatia. Of these I mated with ten in a single night...*

NOTES

52. Chilperic I (c. 539 - September 584) was the King of Neustria (or Soissons) from 561 to his death. He was one of the sons of the Frankish king Clotaire I and Queen Aregund. When the Merovingian king Sigebert married Brunhilda, daughter of the Visigothic sovereign in Spain (Athanagild), Chilperic also wished to make a brilliant marriage. He had already rejected his first wife, Audovera, and had taken as his concubine a serving-woman called Fredegund. He dismissed Fredegund in favour of Brunhilda's sister, Galswintha. But he soon tired of his new partner, and one morning Galswintha was found strangled in her bed. A few days afterwards Chilperic married Fredegund.

53. Xerxes I (519 BC - 465 BC), also called Xerxes the Great, was the fifth king of kings of the Achaemenid dynasty of Persia. Reputed to be driven by blood lust and lust for territory and glory, he ruled from 486 BC until his assassination in 465 BC at the hands of Artabanus, the commander of the royal bodyguard.

54. Bolesław II the Generous, also known as the Bold and the Cruel (c. 1042 - 2 or 3 April 1081 or 1082), was Duke of Poland from 1058 to 1076. According to historical records he 'set out with Virtue and Courage, restoring deposed Princes to their Throne, and Triumphed over Ruffians and Bohemians; but suddenly started from his brave course of honour, to the extremity of effeminacy, in his Ruffian Winter Quarters; which he continued on his return hence to rapes, adulteries etc. and had Stanislaus, Bishop of Cracow, murdered at the Altar, for reprehending him'.

55. Sigismondo Pandolfo Malatesta (19 June 1417 - 7 October 1468) was an Italian condottiero and nobleman, a member of the House of Malatesta and Lord of Rimini, Fano, and Cesena from 1432. Numerous contemporary writers described him as a tyrant and a womaniser who indulged in rape, adultery, and incest.

56. These poems have been translated to make their meaning clearer. The original rhymes have been lost in the process.

MARTIN FIRRELL

The public artist Martin Firrell uses text in public space to promote debate. The more people think about, question and debate a topic, the more likely it becomes that change will occur.

Firrell uses language to engage directly with the public, promoting constructive dialogues, usually about marginalisation, equality and more equitable social organisation, with the aim of making the world more humane. His work has been summarised as 'art as debate'.

Socialart.work is a mass public art project created by Martin Firrell calling for greater social justice. It aims to create debate about power and its abuse, feminism, women's equality and gender, alternative forms of economic and social organisation, black power, counter-culture, and solidarity between people of different backgrounds and ethnicities.

The project includes posters, publications and events supported in 2018-19 by the digital media company Clear Channel UK.

Martin Firrell has been described in the Guardian newspaper as 'one of the capital's most influential public artists'.

More information about this project can be found at www.socialart.work. More information about the artist can be found at Wikipedia.

www.ingramcontent.com/pod-product-compliance
Lightning Source LLC
Chambersburg PA
CBHW020258030426
42336CB00010B/830